Wonderful ways to prepare

PRESSURE COOKER DISHES

by JO ANN SHIRLEY

TITLES AVAILABLE

Wonderful Ways to Prepare
HORS D'OEUVRES & FIRST COURSES
SOUPS
MEAT
FISH & SEAFOOD
STEWS & CASSEROLES
SALADS
DESSERTS
CAKES & COOKIES
BARBECUES
ITALIAN FOOD
CHINESE DISHES
CROCKERY POT DISHES
FOOD FOR FREEZING
PRESERVES
VEGETARIAN DISHES
CALORIE CONTROLLED DISHES
CHEESECAKES
COCKTAILS & MIXED DRINKS
CHICKEN
MEALS IN A WOK
MICROWAVE DISHES
EGGS
PRESSURE COOKER DISHES
ASIAN MEALS
BISCUITS AND COOKIES
CAKES AND SWEETS
CREPES & PANCAKES
BLENDER & MIXER DISHES
FONDUES

Wonderful ways to prepare

PRESSURE COOKER DISHES

PUBLISHED BY
PLAYMORE INC. New York, USA
AND WALDMAN PUBLISHING CORP. New York, USA

AYERS & JAMES
CROWS NEST AUSTRALIA

FIRST PUBLISHED 1983

PUBLISHED BY
PLAYMORE INC. New York, USA
AND WALDMAN PUBLISHING CORP. New York, USA

PUBLISHED IN AUSTRALIA
BY AYERS & JAMES
CROWS NEST. AUSTRALIA

COPYRIGHT 1983
AYERS & JAMES PTY. LTD.
5 ALEXANDER STREET
CROWS NEST N.S.W. AUSTRALIA

PRINTED IN CANADA

ISBN 0 86908-234 5

Contents

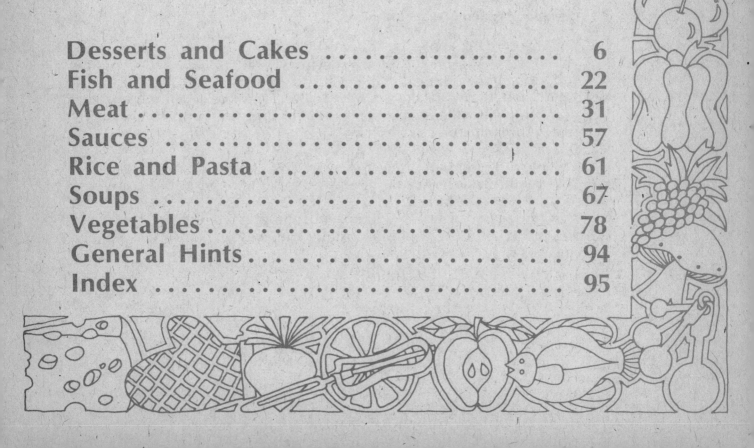

Desserts and Cakes

Brown Betty

1 lb (500 g) cooking apples	1 teaspoon cinnamon
1 cup dry bread crumbs	⅓ cup brown sugar
2 tablespoons raisins	2 tablespoons (40 g) butter
2 tablespoons currants	2 tablespoons molasses
1 tablespoon candied orange and lemon peel	1 tablespoon warm water
1 teaspoon grated orange rind	whipped cream

1. Peel and core the apples and cut into thin slices.
2. Mix together the bread crumbs, raisins, currants, peel, grated orange rind, cinnamon and sugar.
3. Butter and flour a cake pan and layer the bread crumb mixture alternately with the sliced apples. Begin and end with layers of the bread crumb mixture.
4. Dot the butter on top of the last layer.
5. Melt the molasses with the warm water and pour over Brown Betty.
6. Cover with two layers of buttered wax paper and put into the pressure cooker on a rack or trivet.
7. Pour three cups of water (750 ml) into the pressure cooker, cover and pressure cook for ten minutes. Allow the pressure to drop gradually. Uncover and remove the pan.
8. Serve warm or cold with whipped cream.

Serves 4-6.

Gingerbread

1 cup cake flour
1 teaspoon baking soda
1 teaspoon ginger
½ teaspoon cinnamon
⅛ teaspoon salt
2 tablespoons butter
2 tablespoons sugar
2 tablespoons molasses
⅓ cup (85 ml) milk

1 egg

Vanilla Glaze:
2½ tablespoons cream
¼ teaspoon vanilla
1 tablespoon (20 g) butter
1½ cups confectioners' sugar
pinch of salt

1. Sift together the flour, baking soda, ginger, cinnamon and salt into a mixing bowl.
2. Put the butter, sugar and molasses into a small saucepan and heat gently until melted. Pour on the sifted ingredients and beat well.
3. Heat the milk in the same small saucepan, then add to the mixture.
4. Lightly beat the egg, then mix into the gingerbread mixture.
5. Butter and flour a cake pan. Pour in the gingerbread mixture and cover with two layers of buttered wax paper.
6. Pour three cups (750 ml) of water into the pressure cooker. Put the pan on a rack or trivet, cover the cooker and steam for 15 minutes. (Do not put the Pressure Regulator on the Vent Pipe but allow a gentle flow of steam to emerge.) Pressure cook for 25 minutes. Allow the pressure to drop gradually. Remove the lid and allow the gingerbread to stand for 15 minutes before removing from the pan. Put on a wire rack and allow to cool completely.
7. Put all of the Vanilla Glaze ingredients into an electric blender and whirl until smooth. Spread over the cooled gingerbread.

Chocolate Cake

1½ tablespoons molasses
⅓ cup (85 ml) milk
1½ tablespoons (30 g) butter
¾ cup cake flour
½ teaspoon baking soda
1½ tablespoons cocoa
powder

¼ cup sugar
⅛ teaspoon vanilla

Icing:
3 tablespoons confectioners' sugar
⅓ cup melted chocolate
1 tablespoon (20 ml) melted

1. Mix together the molasses, milk and butter in a small saucepan. Stir over a low heat until the butter is melted. Remove from the heat.
2. Sift the flour, baking soda and cocoa into a mixing bowl.
3. Add the sugar and the warm liquid and mix thoroughly.
4. Stir in the vanilla.
5. Butter and flour a cake pan. Pour in the cake mixture and cover with two layers of buttered wax paper.
6. Pour in 3 cups (750 ml) of water into the pressure cooker. Put the cake pan on a rack or trivet, cover the cooker and steam for 15 minutes. (Do not put the Pressure Regulator on the Vent Pipe but allow a gentle flow of steam to emerge.) Pressure cook for 25 minutes. Allow pressure to drop gradually. Uncover and allow the cake to stand for 15 minutes before removing from the pan. Cool completely on a wire rack.
7. Make the icing by mixing together the confectioners' sugar, melted chocolate and melted butter. Pour over the cooled cake while the icing is still liquid.

Rhubarb Brown Betty

4 cups chopped rhubarb
2 tablespoons lemon juice
1 cup quick-cooking rolled oats
⅓ cup flour

½ cup brown sugar
½ teaspoon salt
1 teaspoon cinnamon
⅓ cup (85 ml) melted butter

1. Sprinkle the rhubarb with the lemon juice.
2. Combine the rest of the ingredients.
3. Place alternate layers of the rhubarb and oat mixture, beginning and ending with the oat mixture, in a well-buttered basin. Cover with two layers of buttered wax paper.
4. Pour ½ cup (125 ml) water into the pressure cooker and put the basin on a rack or trivet. Cover and pressure cook for 20 minutes. Reduce the pressure quickly by running cold water over the lid. Uncover and remove the basin. Serve warm or cold. Delicious with warm custard.

Serves 4.

Fruit Cake

1½ cups cake flour
½ cup (125 g) butter
½ cup sugar
⅓ cup raisins

2 tablespoons currants
⅓ cup candied orange and lemon
  peel
1 large egg
milk

1. Sift the flour into a mixing bowl.
2. Add the butter and mix until it resembles fine bread crumbs.
3. Mix in the sugar, raisins, currants and peel.
4. Lightly beat the egg, then add to the mixture with just enough milk to make a thick consistency.
5. Butter and flour a cake pan and spoon in the fruit cake mixture. Cover with two layers of buttered wax paper.
6. Pour three cups (750 ml) of water into the pressure cooker. Put the cake pan on a rack or trivet and cover the pressure cooker.
7. Steam for 15 minutes. (Do not put the Pressure Regulator on the Vent Pipe but allow a gentle flow of steam to emerge.) Pressure cook for 35 minutes. Allow pressure to reduce gradually. Remove from the cooker and let stand for several hours before serving.

Chocolate Pudding Cake

3 tablespoons (60 g) butter
3 tablespoons sugar
2 eggs, separated
⅓ cup cake flour

1½ tablespoons cocoa powder
¾ cup (185 ml) milk
vanilla ice cream

1. Cream together the butter and sugar until light and fluffy.
2. Beat in the egg yolks.
3. Sift together the flour and cocoa powder and fold into the mixture.
4. Slowly add the milk beating constantly.
5. Beat the egg whites until stiff and fold into the mixture.
6. Butter and flour a souffle dish. Pour in the chocolate pudding mixture and cover with two layers of buttered wax paper.
7. Pour 1¼ cups (300 ml) water into the pressure cooker. Put the dish on a rack or trivet, cover and pressure cook for five minutes. Allow the pressure to drop gradually, uncover and serve warm or cold with ice cream.

Serves 4.

Peach Compote

4 large firm peaches	1¼ cups (300 ml) water
3 firm apricots	2 tablespoons apricot jam
6 prunes, pitted	1 tablespoon redcurrant jam
½ cup raisins	2 tablespoons brandy
2 tablespoons orange juice	whipped cream
1 teaspoon grated orange rind	chopped nuts

1. Peel the peaches and apricots. Cut in half and remove the pits. Mix with the prunes and raisins and set aside.
2. Put the orange juice, grated orange rind, water and jams in the pressure cooker and stir over a low heat until the jams are melted.
3. Add the fruit, cover and pressure cook for five minutes. Reduce the pressure quickly by running cold water over the lid. Uncover.
4. Cool slightly, then stir in the brandy.
5. Serve warm or cold with whipped cream and chopped nuts on top.

Serves 4.

Rice Pudding

1 tablespoon (20 g) butter	¼ cup short grain rice
2 cups (500 ml) milk	½ teaspoon vanilla
½ cup (125 ml) cream	⅓ cup raisins
2½ tablespoons sugar	½ teaspoon grated lemon rind

1. Melt the butter in the pressure cooker.
2. Add the milk and bring to the boil.
3. Add the cream, sugar, rice, vanilla, raisins and grated lemon rind. Return the mixture to a boil. Reduce heat and simmer for one minute.
4. Cover and pressure cook for 12 minutes. Allow the pressure to drop gradually. Serve warm or cold.

Serves 4.

Parisian Pudding

⅓ cup sugar
3 tablespoons water
1⅔ cups (415 ml) milk
2 cups soft bread crumbs
⅓ cup chopped glacé
    cherries
2 tablespoons candied orange and
    lemon peel

⅓ cup chopped blanched
    almonds
⅓ cup raisins
2 tablespoons currants
3 eggs
3 teaspoons sugar
whipped cream

1. Mix together the sugar and water in a saucepan. Stir over a low heat until the sugar has dissolved. Then allow it to boil without stirring until it is golden brown.
2. Stirring constantly, add the milk. Cook over a low heat until thoroughly blended.
3. Mix together the bread crumbs, cherries, peel, almonds, raisins and currants in a mixing bowl.
4. Pour the sugared milk over the mixture and stir well.
5. Beat the eggs with the sugar, then mix into the bowl.
6. Butter a souffle dish and pour in the pudding mixture. Cover the dish with two layers of buttered wax paper.
7. Pour 1¼ cups (300 ml) of water into the pressure cooker. Put the dish on a rack or trivet, cover and pressure cook for ten minutes. Allow the pressure to reduce gradually.
8. Uncover the cooker, remove the paper from the dish and serve warm or cold with whipped cream.

Serves 4-6.

Almond Pudding

2 cups soft bread crumbs
2 tablespoons raisins
2 tablespoons candied orange and lemon peel
⅔ cup chopped blanched almonds

1⅔ cups (415 ml) milk
¼ teaspoon vanilla
1 tablespoon sugar
3 eggs

1. Mix together the bread crumbs, raisins, peel and almonds.
2. Heat the milk in a small saucepan. Add the vanilla, then pour into the bread crumb mixture. Mix well.
3. Beat the eggs with the sugar. Add to the pudding mixture.
4. Butter a souffle dish. Pour in the pudding mixture and cover with two layers of buttered wax paper.
5. Pour 1¼ cups (300 ml) of water into the pressure cooker. Put the pudding on a rack or trivet, cover and pressure cook for ten minutes. Allow the pressure to reduce gradually. Uncover and remove the almond pudding. Serve warm or cold.

Serves 4-6.

Bread and Butter Pudding

4 slices day-old bread
butter
raisins
candied orange and lemon peel

3 eggs
⅛ teaspoon vanilla
2 tablespoons sugar
1¾ cups (435 ml) milk

1. Cut the crusts from the bread and butter generously. Cut into triangles.
2. Butter a dish and put a layer of buttered bread on the bottom. Sprinkle on raisins and peel. Continue layering ending with bread.
3. Lightly beat the eggs with the vanilla.
4. Heat the sugar with the milk stirring over a low heat until the sugar dissolves. Slowly pour over the egg mixture, stirring constantly.
5. Pour the custard mixture over the bread. Allow to stand for 15 minutes. Cover with two layers of buttered wax paper.
6. Pour 1¼ cups (300 ml) water into the pressure cooker. Put the dish on a rack or trivet and cover.
7. Pressure cook for ten minutes. Allow the pressure to drop gradually. Uncover and remove the dish. Take off the paper and serve warm with cream.

Serves 4-6.

Orange Custard

3 eggs
1 egg yolk
⅛ teaspoon vanilla
2 tablespoons sugar
1 cup (250 ml) milk

¾ cup (185 ml) cream
1½ teaspoons grated orange rind
1 tablespoon Cointreau
ice cream

1. Lightly beat the eggs and egg yolk with the vanilla.
2. Heat the sugar with the milk, stirring over a low heat until the sugar dissolves. Slowly pour into the egg mixture, stirring constantly.
3. Add the cream, orange rind and Cointreau.
4. Butter a souffle or custard dish. Pour in the custard mixture which should not fill the dish more than three-quarters.
5. Cover the dish with two layers of buttered wax paper.
6. Pour 1¼ cups (300 ml) of water into the pressure cooker. Put the dish on a rack or trivet and cover.
7. Pressure cook for five minutes. Allow the pressure to drop gradually. Remove the lid and take the paper off. Serve warm or cold with ice cream.

Serves 4.

Egg Custard

3 eggs
⅛ teaspoon vanilla
2 tablespoons sugar
1⅔ cups (415 ml) milk
nutmeg

1. Lightly beat the eggs with the vanilla.
2. Heat together the sugar and milk. Slowly pour into the egg mixture, stirring constantly.
3. Butter a souffle or custard dish. Pour in the mixture which should not fill the dish more than three-quarters. Sprinkle on a little nutmeg.
4. Cover the dish with two layers of buttered wax paper.
5. Pour 1¼ cups (300 ml) of water into the pressure cooker. Put the dish on a rack or trivet and cover.
6. Pressure cook for five minutes. Allow the pressure to drop gradually. Remove the lid and take the paper off. Serve warm or cold.

Serves 4.

Rich Egg Custard

3 eggs
2 egg yolks
⅛ teaspoon vanilla
2 tablespoons sugar
1¾ cups (435 ml) milk
nutmeg or cinnamon

1. Lightly beat the eggs and egg yolks with the vanilla.
2. Heat the sugar with the milk then slowly pour into the egg mixture, stirring constantly.
3. Butter a souffle or custard dish. Pour in the mixture which should not fill the dish more than three-quarters full. Sprinkle on a little nutmeg or cinnamon.
4. Cover the dish with two layers of buttered wax paper.
5. Pour 1¼ cups (300 ml) water into the pressure cooker. Put the dish on a rack or trivet and cover.
6. Pressure cook for five minutes. Allow the pressure to drop gradually. Remove the lid and take the paper off. Serve warm or cold.

Serves 4.

Rice Pudding Parfait

1 tablespoon (20 g) butter
2 cups (500 ml) milk
½ cup (125 ml) cream
2½ tablespoons sugar
¼ cup short grain rice

½ teaspoon vanilla
½ teaspoon grated lemon rind
1 cup mashed raspberries
whipped cream
crushed nuts

1. Melt the butter in the pressure cooker.
2. Add the milk and bring to a boil.
3. Add the cream, sugar, rice, vanilla and lemon rind.
4. Return to a boil. Reduce heat and simmer for one minute, stirring constantly.
5. Cover and pressure cook for 12 minutes. Allow the pressure to drop gradually. Remove the lid.
6. Spoon a little of the pudding into a parfait glass. Put a little of the mashed raspberries on top. Continue layering ending with the rice pudding.
7. Top with whipped cream and crushed nuts. Serve hot or cold.

Serves 4.

Steamed Mocha Pudding

½ cup (125 g) butter	2 teaspoons instant coffee powder
½ cup sugar	2 teaspoons cocoa powder
2 large eggs	2 tablespoons hot water
1¼ cups cake flour	Coffee Sauce

1. Cream together the butter and sugar until light and fluffy.
2. Add the eggs one at a time beating well after each addition.
3. Sift the flour over the mixing bowl and gently fold in.
4. Blend the coffee powder, cocoa powder and water. Stir into the pudding mix.
5. Butter and flour a four-cup (one-liter) basin and pour in the pudding mixture.
6. Butter a piece of wax paper and put on top of the basin, butter side down. Make a pleat in the paper to allow for expansion. Tie with a piece of string.
7. Put the basin on a rack or trivet in the pressure cooker and pour in four cups (one liter) of water.
8. Steam for 15 minutes. (Do not put the Pressure Regulator on the Vent Pipe but allow a gentle flow of steam to emerge.) Then pressure cook for 25 minutes. Allow the pressure to reduce gradually.
9. Uncover the cooker and turn out the pudding. Serve warm with Coffee Sauce.

Serves 4.

Coffee Sauce:
1½ tablespoons cornstarch
2 tablespoons sugar
½ cup (125 ml) strong coffee
½ cup (125 ml) milk
2 tablespoons cream
1 tablespoon (20 g) butter

Blend together the cornstarch, sugar and half the coffee in a small saucepan. Add the rest of the ingredients and cook over a low heat, stirring constantly, until thickened.

Steamed Golden Pudding

½ cup (125 g) butter
½ cup sugar
2 large eggs
1¼ cups cake flour

1 teaspoon grated orange rind
½ teaspoon grated lemon rind
¼ cup (65 ml) molasses
warm custard

1. Cream together the butter and sugar until light and fluffy.
2. Add the eggs one at a time beating well after each addition.
3. Sift the flour over the mixing bowl and gently fold in.
4. Stir in the orange and lemon rind.
5. Butter and flour a four-cup (one-liter) basin.
6. Pour the molasses on the bottom of the basin then pour in the pudding mixture.
7. Butter a piece of wax paper and put it on top of the basin, butter side down. Make a pleat in the paper to allow for expansion. Tie with a piece of string.
8. Put the basin on a rack or trivet in the pressure cooker and pour in four cups (one liter) of water.
9. Steam for 15 minutes. (Do not put the Pressure Regulator on the Vent Pipe but allow a gentle flow of steam to emerge.) Then pressure cook for 25 minutes. Allow the pressure to reduce gradually.
10. Uncover and turn out the pudding. Serve warm with custard.

Serves 4.

Pears in Red Wine

6 large firm pears
rind of one orange, cut into thin
    strips
1½ tablespoons orange juice
½ cup (125 ml) water

⅔ cup (165 ml) red wine
2 tablespoons sugar
2 tablespoons plum jam
slivered blanched almonds
cream

1. Peel the pears. Cut in half and remove the cores.
2. Put the orange rind strips, orange juice, water, red wine and sugar into the pressure cooker. Heat gently until the sugar is dissolved.
3. Put the pear halves in the cooker, cover and pressure cook for five minutes. Reduce the pressure quickly by running cold water over the lid. Uncover.
4. Put the pears onto a serving dish.
5. Stir the plum jam into the syrup until it dissolves.
6. Remove the orange rind strips and pour the syrup over the pears.
7. Serve warm or cold with slivered almonds and cream.

Serves 4-6.

Steamed Fruit Pudding

½ cup (125 g) butter
½ cup sugar
2 large eggs
1¼ cups cake flour
3 tablespoons raisins
1 tablespoon candied orange and
   lemon peel

2 tablespoons currants
2 tablespoons chopped peaches
2 tablespoons chopped apples
1 teaspoon grated lemon rind
1 teaspoon grated orange rind
whipped cream or custard

1. Cream together the butter and sugar until light and fluffy.
2. Add the eggs one at a time beating well after each addition.
3. Sift the flour over the mixing bowl and gently fold in.
4. Add the raisins, peel and currants. Blend thoroughly.
5. Butter and flour a four-cup (one-liter) basin.
6. Mix together the peaches, apples, lemon and orange rinds. Spread on the bottom of the basin.
7. Pour in the pudding mixture.
8. Butter a piece of wax paper and put on top of the basin, butter side down. Make a pleat in the paper to allow for expansion. Tie with a piece of string.
9. Put the basin on a rack or trivet in the pressure cooker and pour in four cups (one liter) of water.
10. Steam for 15 minutes. (Do not put the Pressure Regulator on the Vent Pipe but allow a gentle flow of steam to emerge.) Then pressure cook for 25 minutes. Allow the pressure to reduce gradually.
11. Uncover the cooker and turn out the pudding. Serve warm with whipped cream or custard.

Serves 4.

Steamed Sponge Pudding

½ cup (125 g) butter　　　　1¼ cups cake flour
½ cup sugar　　　　　　　　whipped cream or ice
2 large eggs　　　　　　　　cream

1. Cream together the butter and sugar until light and fluffy.
2. Add the eggs one at a time beating well after each addition.
3. Sift the flour over the mixing bowl and gently fold in.
4. Butter and flour a 4-cup (1-liter) basin and pour in the mixture.
5. Butter a piece of wax paper and put on top of the basin, butter side down. Make a pleat in the paper to allow for expansion. Tie with a piece of string.
6. Put the basin on a rack or trivet in the pressure cooker and pour in 4 cups (1 liter) of water.
7. Steam for 15 minutes. (Do not put the Pressure Regulator on the Vent Pipe but allow a gentle flow of steam to emerge.) Then pressure cook for 25 minutes. Allow the pressure to reduce gradually.
8. Uncover the pressure cooker and turn out the sponge pudding. Serve warm with whipped cream or ice cream.

Serves 4.

Steamed Raspberry Pudding

½ cup (125 g) butter　　　　1¼ cups cake flour
½ cup sugar　　　　　　　　⅔ cup fresh or canned raspberries
2 large eggs　　　　　　　　warm custard

1. Cream together the butter and sugar until light and fluffy.
2. Add the eggs one at a time beating well after each addition.
3. Sift the flour over the mixing bowl and gently fold in.
4. Butter and flour a 4-cup (1-liter) basin and put in the raspberries. Pour in the sponge mixture.
5. Butter a piece of wax paper and put on top of the basin, butter side down. Make a pleat in the paper to allow for expansion. Tie with a piece of string.
6. Put the basin on a rack or trivet in the pressure cooker and pour in 4 cups (1 liter) of water.
7. Steam for 15 minutes. (Do not put the Pressure Regulator on the Vent Pipe but allow a gentle flow of steam to emerge.) Then pressure cook for 25 minutes. Allow the pressure to reduce gradually.
8. Uncover the pressure cooker and turn out the pudding. Serve warm with custard.

Serves 4.

Steamed Chocolate Pudding

½ cup (125 g) butter
½ cup sugar
2 large eggs

1¼ cups cake flour
1½ tablespoons cocoa powder
Chocolate Sauce

1. Cream together the butter and sugar until light and fluffy.
2. Add the eggs one at a time beating well after each addition.
3. Sift the flour with the cocoa powder and gently fold in.
4. Butter and flour a four-cup (one-liter) basin and pour in the mixture.
5. Butter a piece of wax paper and put on top of the basin, butter side down. Make a pleat in the paper to allow for expansion. Tie with a piece of string.
6. Put the basin on a rack or trivet in the pressure cooker and pour in four cups (one liter) of water.
7. Steam for 15 minutes. (Do not put the Pressure Regulator on the Vent Pipe but allow a gentle flow of steam to emerge.) Then pressure cook for 25 minutes. Allow the pressure to reduce gradually.
8. Uncover the pressure cooker and turn out the pudding. Serve with Chocolate Sauce.

Serves 4.

Chocolate Sauce:
1 tablespoon cornstarch
1 tablespoon cocoa powder
2½ tablespoons sugar
1¼ cups (300 ml) milk
1½ tablespoons (30 g) butter

Mix together the cornstarch, cocoa and sugar in a small saucepan. Slowly add the milk, stirring constantly. Heat gently, then add the butter and, stirring constantly, cook over a low heat until thick and smooth.

Christmas Pudding

1 cooking apple, peeled and grated
1 medium carrot, peeled and grated
½ cup ground blanched almonds
2 teaspoons grated lemon rind
⅓ cup (85 ml) lemon juice
½ cup cake flour
1 teaspoon mixed spice
½ teaspoon nutmeg
1 teaspoon cinnamon

2 cups soft bread crumbs
⅔ cup brown sugar
½ cup (125 ml) melted butter
1½ tablespoons molasses
2 cups raisins
⅔ cup currants
⅓ cup candied orange and lemon peel
½ cup chopped glacé cherries
2 large eggs
½ cup (125 ml) beer or brandy

1. Thoroughly mix together all the ingredients. Allow to stand for several hours or overnight before cooking.
2. Butter and flour two medium basins (as this mixture gives enough for two puddings). Divide the mixture between the two basins. Cover with buttered wax paper or muslin. Tie on with string.
3. Put the basin on a rack or trivet in the pressure cooker. Pour in 4 cups (one liter) of water. Cover and steam for 20 minutes. (Do not put the Pressure Regulator on the Vent Pipe but allow a gentle flow of steam to emerge.) Then pressure cook for 2¼ hours. Allow the pressure to drop gradually.
4. Remove the pudding from the cooker, take off the covering and allow to cool. Store until ready to use. Before serving, return to the pressure cooker with 4 cups of water and pressure cook for ½ hour. Allow the pressure to reduce gradually, then uncover. Turn out and serve the pudding with Brandy Butter.

Brandy Butter: Mix together ¾ cup (185 g) butter and 1½ cups sifted confectioners' sugar. Beat in ⅓ cup (85 ml) brandy. Chill and serve with the pudding.

Light Christmas Pudding

¼ lb (125 g) carrots, grated
¼ lb (125 g) apples, weighed when grated
2 cups raisins
⅓ cup currants
4 cups soft bread crumbs
1 cup cake flour
1½ teaspoons grated lemon rind

½ teaspoon mixed spice
½ teaspoon nutmeg
½ teaspoon cinnamon
½ cup (125 ml) melted butter
1 cup brown sugar
1½ tablespoons molasses
⅓ cup (85 ml) milk
1 large egg
warm custard

1. Thoroughly mix together all the ingredients.
2. Prepare the basin by greasing well. Pour in the mixture. Butter a piece of wax paper. Put on top of the pudding, buttered side down, with a pleat in it to allow for expansion. Tie on with string.
3. Pour four cups (one liter) of water into the pressure cooker. Put the basin on a rack or trivet to keep the basin above the water.
4. Cover and steam for 20 minutes. (To steam, do not put the Pressure Regulator on the Vent Pipe but allow a gentle flow of steam to emerge.) Pressure cook for 2¼ hours. Allow the pressure to reduce gradually. If not eaten immediately, pressure cook for ½ hour before serving. Serve with warm custard.

Lemon Pudding Cake

3 tablespoons (60 g) butter
3 tablespoons sugar
3 teaspoons grated lemon rind
2 eggs, separated

⅓ cup cake flour
½ cup (125 ml) milk
¼ cup (65 ml) lemon juice
whipped cream

1. Cream together the butter and sugar until light and fluffy.
2. Add the grated lemon rind and eggs yolks and beat well.
3. Sift the flour and fold into the mixture.
4. Add the milk, then the lemon juice.
5. Beat the egg whites until stiff, then fold into the lemon mixture.
6. Butter and flour a souffle dish. Pour in the lemon pudding mixture and cover with two layers of buttered wax paper.
7. Pour 1¼ cups (300 ml) of water into the pressure cooker. Put the dish on a rack or trivet, cover and pressure cook for five minutes. Allow the pressure to drop gradually, uncover and serve warm or cold with whipped cream.

Serves 4.

Fish and Seafood

Sour Sole

2 medium onions, sliced
1 lb (500 g) fillet of sole
1 teaspoon pickling spice
1 teaspoon brown sugar
⅔ cup (165 ml) water
⅔ cup (165 ml) vinegar

1. Put the slices of onions on the bottom of the pressure cooker.
2. Arrange the fish on top of the onions.
3. Mix together the pickling spice, sugar, water and vinegar. Pour over the fish.
4. Cover and pressure cook for two minutes. Reduce the pressure rapidly by running cold water over the lid.

Serves 4.

Flounder with Grapes

1 lb (500 g) flounder
1¼ cups (300 ml) fish stock
salt and pepper
½ lb (250 g) seedless grapes,
   skinned

1½ tablespoons (30 g) butter
1½ tablespoons flour
¼ cup (65 ml) cream
chopped parsley

1. Put the fish into the pressure cooker with the fish stock, salt and pepper to taste and the grapes. Cover and pressure cook for three minutes.
2. Put the fish on a serving dish and keep warm.
3. Pour the grapes and the liquid from the cooker into an electric blender and whirl until smooth.
4. Melt the butter in the open cooker. Stir in the flour and cook for ½ minute. Slowly stir in the puréed grapes. Cook over a medium heat, stirring constantly, until thickened. Remove from the heat and season to taste with salt and pepper.
5. Stir the cream into the sauce, then pour over the fish.
6. Serve garnished with chopped parsley.

Serves 4.

Smoked Haddock

1 lb (500 g) smoked haddock
⅔ cup (165 ml) milk
⅔ cup (165 ml) water
2 teaspoons chopped fresh dill
1 lemon sliced

1. Put the fish in the pressure cooker with the milk, water, dill and lemon slices.
2. Cover and pressure cook for three minutes. Allow pressure to drop gradually.

Serves 4.

Fish Curry

1 medium onion, minced
1 cooking apple, peeled, cored
  and grated
1 clove garlic, minced
3 tablespoons (60 g) butter
2 teaspoons curry powder (or to
  taste)
2 tablespoons raisins

1¼ cups (300 ml) water
2 teaspoons lemon juice
½ teaspoon sugar
salt and pepper
1 lb (500 g) flounder fillets
2 tablespoons flour
⅔ cup (165 ml) milk
cooked white rice

1. Sauté the onion, apple and garlic in the butter in the open pressure cooker for three minutes, stirring frequently.
2. Add the curry powder, mix well and cook for another minute.
3. Stir in the raisins, water, lemon juice, sugar and salt and pepper to taste. Bring to the boil. Reduce the heat and simmer for five minutes.
4. Add the fish, cover and pressure cook for two minutes.
5. Reduce the pressure rapidly by running cold water over the lid of the cooker. Remove the lid.
6. Blend the flour with the milk. Stir into the curry sauce and bring to the boil. Reduce heat and simmer for two minutes.
7. Serve over hot cooked rice.

Serves 4.

Tuna Nicoise

4 pieces tuna steak
salt and pepper
4 teaspoons lemon juice
3 tablespoons (60 g) butter
4 small tomatoes

2 teaspoons chopped tarragon
4 teaspoons chopped parsley
2 teaspoons grated lemon rind
8 anchovy fillets
16 olives, halved and pitted

1. Season each steak with salt and pepper to taste and sprinkle with a teaspoon of lemon juice. Set aside for ½ hour.
2. Melt the butter in a skillet and brown the tuna on both sides. Put the steaks on a heat-proof dish. Pour on any butter from the skillet.
3. Slice the tomatoes and put on top of the fish.
4. Sprinkle on the tarragon, parsley, lemon rind, anchovy fillets and olives.
5. Pour 1¼ cups (300 ml) water into the pressure cooker. Put the fish dish on a rack or trivet, cover and pressure cook for three minutes. Allow the pressure to reduce gradually.

Serves 4.

Fish Meuniere

¼ cup (65 g) butter
1 lb (500 g) white fish fillets
2 tablespoons (40 g) butter
¼ cup (65 ml) lemon juice

¼ cup chopped parsley
⅓ cup capers
lemon wedges

1. Melt the butter in a skillet and brown the fish on both sides. Transfer to a shallow heat-proof dish.
2. Melt the rest of the butter in the skillet and stir in the lemon juice, parsley and capers. Bring to a simmer, then pour over the fish.
3. Pour 1¼ cups (300 ml) water into the pressure cooker. Place the dish of fish on a rack or trivet, cover and pressure cook for three minutes.
4. Serve with lemon wedges.

Serves 4.

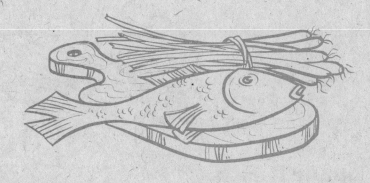

Fish au Gratin

1 lb (500 g) fish fillets
¼ cup grated Parmesan cheese
¼ cup grated Cheddar cheese
¼ cup dried bread crumbs
¼ cup (65 ml) melted butter
chopped chives

1. Butter a large piece of aluminum foil. Put on the fish, fold up and seal.
2. Pour 1¼ cups (300 ml) water into the pressure cooker. Put the fish on a rack or trivet. Cover and pressure cook for four minutes. Allow pressure to reduce gradually. Remove the fish from the cooker and open the foil. Place on a broiler rack.
3. Mix together the Parmesan and Cheddar cheese, bread crumbs and melted butter. Spread on top of the fish and put under a hot broiler until golden brown.
4. Serve garnished with chopped chives.

Serves 4.

Trout Amandine

3 tablespoons (60 g) butter
4 fresh trout
1 cup slivered blanched almonds

1. Melt the butter in a skillet and brown the trout on both sides.
2. Transfer the fish to a heat-proof dish.
3. Fry the almonds in the skillet for two minutes. Spoon over the fish.
4. Pour one cup (250 ml) water into the pressure cooker. Place the dish of fish on a rack or trivet, cover and pressure cook for three minutes. Allow the pressure to drop gradually.

Serves 4.

Spanish Fish

3 cloves garlic, minced
3 medium onions, chopped
6 tomatoes, chopped
1 sweet green pepper, chopped
salt and black pepper

3 tablespoons (60 ml) melted butter
1 lb (500 g) fish fillets
lemon wedges

1. Mix together the garlic, onions, tomatoes and pepper.
2. Season to taste with salt and pepper, then stir in the melted butter.
3. Spread half the mixture on the bottom of a casserole dish.
4. Arrange the fish on top then spread on the remaining mixture.
5. Butter a piece of aluminum foil and cover the casserole dish.
6. Pour 1¼ cups (300 ml) water into the pressure cooker. Place the casserole dish on a rack or trivet, cover and pressure cook for five minutes. Allow the pressure to drop gradually. Serve with lemon wedges.

Serves 4.

Fish with Fennel Sauce

⅔ cup (165 ml) cream
1 teaspoon American mustard
¼ teaspoon salt
¼ teaspoon black pepper

2 tablespoons chopped fennel
1 lb (500 g) fish fillets
chopped parsley
lemon wedges

1. Mix together the cream, mustard, salt, pepper and fennel.
2. Butter a casserole dish and arrange the fish on the bottom.
3. Pour the fennel mixture on top.
4. Cover with buttered aluminum foil.
5. Pour 1¼ cups (300 ml) water into the pressure cooker and place the casserole dish on a rack or trivet. Cover and pressure cook for four minutes. Allow the pressure to reduce gradually. Serve with lemon wedges.

Serves 4.

Fish with Anchovy Sauce

1½ lb (750 g) fish fillets
3 tablespoons (60 g) butter
4 anchovy fillets, minced
1 tablespoon minced parsley
¼ teaspoon black pepper
1 teaspoon grated lemon rind

1. Put the fish on one or two pieces of aluminum foil.
2. Mix together the butter, anchovies, parsley, pepper and grated lemon rind.
3. Spread on the fish on both sides. Fold up the foil and seal.
4. Pour 1¼ cups (300 ml) water into the pressure cooker.
5. Place the fish on a rack or trivet. Cover the cooker and pressure cook for four minutes. Reduce the pressure by running cold water on the lid of the cooker.

Serves 4-6.

Fish with Onions and Bacon

4 medium onions, thinly sliced
½ lb (250 g) bacon, chopped
1 lb (500 g) white fish fillets
⅓ cup (85 ml) white wine

1 tablespoon lemon juice
2 tablespoons chopped parsley
1 large potato, thinly sliced
salt and black pepper

1. Butter a casserole dish. Arrange half the onions on the bottom and sprinkle with half the bacon.
2. Put the fish on top and pour on the wine and lemon juice.
3. Place the rest of the onions and bacon on the fish and sprinkle with the chopped parsley.
4. Arrange the potato slices on top and season to taste with salt and pepper.
5. Butter a piece of aluminum foil and cover the casserole dish.
6. Pour 1¼ cups (300 ml) water into the pressure cooker. Place the casserole dish on a rack or trivet, cover and pressure cook for 12 minutes. Allow the pressure to reduce gradually.

Serves 4.

Fish with Tomatoes

2 small onions, chopped
4 medium tomatoes, chopped
2 tablespoons chopped parsley
1 tablespoon chopped chives

¼ cup soft bread crumbs
salt
freshly ground black pepper
1 lb (500 g) fish fillets

1. Mix together the onions, tomatoes, parsley, chives, bread crumbs and salt and pepper to taste.
2. Put half the mixture on the bottom of a buttered casserole dish.
3. Arrange the fish on top, then cover with the rest of the tomato mixture.
4. Put the casserole dish on a rack in the pressure cooker.
5. Pour in 1¼ cups (300 ml) water, cover and pressure cook for five minutes. Allow the pressure to reduce gradually.

Serves 4.

Fish with Bananas

4 fish steaks
2 tablespoons (40 ml) melted
   butter
4 sugar bananas
salt and black pepper
2 teaspoons lemon juice
1 teaspoon grated lemon rind

1. Brush the fish with the melted butter and place each piece on aluminum foil.
2. Cut each banana in half lengthwise and lay on top of the fish.
3. Season to taste with salt and pepper. Sprinkle with the lemon juice and lemon rind.
4. Fold up the foil and seal.
5. Pour 1¼ cups (300 ml) water into the pressure cooker.
6. Put the wrapped fish on a rack or trivet and cover the cooker. Pressure cook for four minutes. Reduce the pressure by running cold water on the lid of the cooker.

Serves 4.

Shrimp with Caraway Seeds

1½ lb (750 g) raw shrimp,
   unshelled
2 cups (500 ml) boiling water
1 teaspoon salt
½ teaspoon freshly ground black
   pepper
1½ tablespoons caraway seeds
2½ tablespoons lemon juice

1. Put the shrimp on a rack or trivet in the pressure cooker.
2. Pour in the water then add the salt, pepper, caraway seeds and lemon juice.
3. Cover and pressure cook just until the pressure regulator begins to rock. Reduce the pressure rapidly by running cold water over the lid.
4. Open the cooker and drain the shrimp. Remove the shells and de-vein.

Serves 3-4.

Shrimp Jambalaya

¼ cup (65 g) bacon fat
2 cloves garlic, minced
1 large onion, chopped
½ lb (250 g) ham, diced
1 cup long grain rice
2 teaspoons salt
¼ teaspoon black pepper
⅛ teaspoon cayenne pepper

¼ teaspoon chili powder
⅛ teaspoon basil
½ cup (125 ml) water
1 can (1 lb) tomatoes
¼ lb (125 g) fresh mushrooms, sliced
1 lb (500 g) cooked peeled shrimp
½ sweet green pepper, sliced

1. Melt the bacon fat in the open pressure cooker and sauté the garlic and onion until golden brown.
2. Add the ham and rice and cook over a medium heat, stirring constantly, until the rice is golden.
3. Stir in the salt, pepper, cayenne pepper, chili powder, basil, water, tomatoes and mushrooms.
4. Put the shrimp and green pepper on top.
5. Cover and pressure cook for five minutes. Reduce the pressure rapidly by running cold water over the lid.
6. Remove the cover and stir well. Allow the Jambalaya to stand for a few minutes before serving.

Serves 6-8.

Steamed Crabs

2 fresh crabs with shells
1 cup (250 ml) boiling water
1 teaspoon salt
3 teaspoons lemon juice
1 onion, sliced
1 bay leaf

1. Put the crabs in boiling water to cover. Drain.
2. Place the crabs on a rack or trivet in the pressure cooker.
3. Add the one cup of boiling water, salt, lemon juice, onion and bay leaf.
4. Cover and pressure cook for five minutes. Reduce the pressure by running cold water over the lid. Serve immediately.

Serves 2.

Meat

Beef with Sour Cream

2 lb (1 kg) bottom round, cut into small cubes
¼ cup (65 ml) vegetable oil
2 tablespoons flour
1 medium onion, chopped
1 stalk celery, chopped
1 clove garlic, minced

1 sweet green pepper, chopped
¼ lb (125 g) fresh mushrooms, sliced
3 tablespoons tomato paste
1 tablespoon Worcestershire sauce
1½ cups (375 g) sour cream
salt and black pepper

1. Brown the beef in the oil in the open pressure cooker.
2. Add the flour and mix well.
3. Stir in the onion, celery, garlic, pepper, mushrooms, tomato paste and Worcestershire sauce. Combine thoroughly.
4. Stir in the sour cream. Season to taste with salt and pepper.
5. Cover and pressure cook for ten minutes.
6. Reduce the pressure by placing the pressure cooker under running cold water. When the pressure has dropped, remove the cover and serve.

Serves 6.

Pork Chop Dinner

4 large pork chops	2 tablespoons vegetable oil
½ cup flour	½ cup (125 ml) water
1 teaspoon salt	2 medium sweet potatoes, halved
1 tablespoon paprika	4 cooking apples, cored

1. Dredge the pork chops in the flour mixed with salt and paprika.
2. Heat the oil in the open pressure cooker and brown the chops on both sides.
3. Add the water, cover and pressure cook for ten minutes.
4. Reduce the pressure by placing the cooker under cold running water.
5. When the pressure has dropped, remove the cover and, arrange the sweet potatoes and apples on top of the chops.
6. Cover and pressure cook for five minutes.
7. Again, reduce the pressure rapidly by placing under cold running water.

Serves 4.

Chop Suey

½ lb (250 g) lean pork, diced	1½ teaspoons sugar
1 lb (500 g) boneless sirloin steak, diced	2½ tablespoons soy sauce
1½ tablespoons vegetable oil	1 cup (250 ml) beef stock
1 teaspoon salt	½ lb (250 g) bean sprouts
¼ teaspoon black pepper	2 tablespoons cornstarch
3 medium onions, chopped	⅔ cup (165 ml) water
½ sweet green pepper, chopped	fried noodles

1. Brown the meats in the oil in the open pressure cooker.
2. Add the salt, pepper, onions, green pepper, sugar, soy sauce and beef stock. Mix well.
3. Cover and pressure cook for ten minutes. Allow pressure to drop gradually.
4. When the pressure has reduced, stir in the bean sprouts.
5. Blend the cornstarch with the water and stir into the Chop Suey.
6. Cook over a low heat, stirring constantly, until thickened.
7. Serve over fried noodles.

Serves 6.

Chinese Pork Chops

4 large pork chops	¼ teaspoon black pepper
1 medium onion, minced	¼ teaspoon ginger
1 can (1 lb) pineapple rings	½ cup (125 ml) beef stock
3 teaspoons German mustard	2 tablespoons cornstarch
1 teaspoon salt	1½ tablespoons soy sauce

1. Cut all the fat from the pork. Heat the pressure cooker and fry a little of the fat to grease the bottom. Remove the fat.
2. Brown the chops on both sides. Remove from the cooker.
3. Add the onions and cook until golden brown.
4. Return the chops to the cooker and add the pineapple rings.
5. Blend together the mustard, salt, pepper, ginger, stock and liquid from the pineapple can. Pour over the chops.
6. Cover and pressure cook for eight minutes. Allow the pressure to drop gradually.
7. Remove the cover and put the chops and pineapple on a warm serving platter.
8. Blend the cornstarch with the soy sauce and a little of the liquid from the cooker, then stir into the sauce. Cook until thickened and clear. Pour over the chops and pineapple and serve immediately.

Serves 4.

New Hampshire Boiled Dinner

4 lb (2 kg) corned brisket of beef	6 medium carrots, scraped
6 small beets	½ cabbage
4 small turnips, peeled	8 potatoes, peeled, quartered

1. Put the beef into the pressure cooker and cover with water. Bring to a boil, then simmer for ten minutes. (Do not put the lid on.)
2. Pour off the water and cover with fresh water. Cover and pressure cook for one hour. Allow the pressure to drop gradually.
3. Open the pressure cooker and add the vegetables. (The beets should not be peeled. Peel them after the dish is cooked.) Cover and pressure cook for eight minutes. Reduce the pressure rapidly by running cold water over the lid.
4. Serve with white sauce and mustard.

Serves 8.

Chicken Marengo

3 lb (1½ kg) chicken pieces
⅓ cup flour
1 teaspoon salt
1 teaspoon black pepper
¼ cup (65 ml) vegetable oil
2 cloves garlic, minced

½ lb (250 g) fresh mushrooms, sliced
1 lb (500 g) very ripe tomatoes, quartered
1 cup (250 ml) dry white wine

1. Wet the chicken pieces with water.
2. Mix together the flour, salt and pepper. Coat the chicken shaking off any excess flour.
3. Heat the vegetable oil in the open pressure cooker and sauté the garlic until golden brown.
4. Add the chicken and brown on all sides. Remove the chicken.
5. Add the mushrooms, tomatoes and half the wine. Mix well.
6. Return the chicken to the cooker, cover and pressure cook for ten minutes. Allow the pressure to drop gradually. Open and remove the chicken. Keep warm on a serving platter.
7. Mix the left-over flour with the remaining white wine then stir into the sauce in the cooker. Cook, stirring constantly, until thickened. Pour over the chicken and serve immediately.

Serves 4.

Beef Stew with wine

2 lb (1 kg) boned beef chuck, cut into cubes
2 medium onions, sliced
3 medium carrots, sliced
½ cup chopped parsley
1½ teaspoons salt

10 whole black peppercorns
⅔ cup (165 ml) red wine
⅓ cup (85 ml) tomato purée
1 tablespoon cornstarch
3 tablespoons water
cooked noodles, hot

1. Put the onions, carrots and parsley into the pressure cooker in layers.
2. Arrange the meat on top.
3. Mix together the salt, peppercorns, wine and tomato purée. Pour over the meat.
4. Cover and pressure cook for ½ hour. Reduce the pressure rapidly by running cold water over the lid. Remove the top and skim off any fat.
5. Blend the cornstarch with the water and stir into the stew. Cook, stirring constantly, until thickened.
6. Serve over hot noodles.

Serves 6.

Beef Stew with Cabbage

2 lb (1 kg) stewing beef, cut into cubes
2 tablespoons vegetable oil
2 cloves garlic, minced
1 large onion, chopped
2 medium carrots, sliced
1 stalk celery, sliced
4 medium tomatoes, chopped
½ sweet green pepper, chopped
2 bay leaves

1 cup barley
2 teaspoons salt
½ teaspoon black pepper
½ teaspoon marjoram
¼ cup (65 g) butter
1 cup chopped scallions
1 tablespoon flour
½ cabbage, shredded
3 cups diced potatoes
½ cup chopped parsley

1. Brown the beef in the vegetable oil in the open pressure cooker.
2. Add the garlic, onion, carrots, celery, tomatoes, pepper, bay leaves, barley, salt, pepper and marjoram. Mix thoroughly.
3. Pour in enough water to cover (but remember that the pressure cooker should not be more than ⅔ full).
4. Cover and pressure cook for 20 minutes. Allow the pressure to reduce gradually.
5. Melt the butter in a large saucepan. Add the scallions and cook over a low heat for three minutes.
6. Stir in the flour. Cook until brown.
7. Add the cabbage, mix well, cover and cook over a low heat for 15 minutes.
8. Add the potatoes and parsley to the stew and simmer in the open pressure cooker until the potatoes are tender.

Serves 6.

Chinese Meat Balls

1 lb (500 g) ground pork	1 large egg
2½ tablespoons soy sauce	3 tablespoons cornstarch
1 tablespoon dry sherry	⅓ cup (85 ml) water
1 scallion, green and white part	5 cups coarsely chopped cabbage
3 slices fresh ginger	½ teaspoon sugar
1 clove garlic, halved	1 tablespoon soy sauce
4 water chestnuts	⅓ cup (85 ml) chicken stock

1. Put the soy sauce, sherry, scallion, ginger, garlic, water chestnuts and egg in an electric blender and whirl until all is well-chopped.
2. Blend together the cornstarch and water. Add 1½ tablespoons of this mixture to the mixture in the blender and whirl until well-mixed.
3. Add this to the ground pork, then shape into about six balls.
4. Dip the pork balls into the rest of the cornstarch mixture then brown in a little oil in a skillet.
5. Put half the cabbage on the bottom of the pressure cooker. Arrange the pork balls on top then top with the rest of the cabbage.
6. Mix together the sugar, soy sauce and chicken stock. Sprinkle over the cabbage.
7. Cover and pressure cook for 20 minutes. Reduce the pressure rapidly by running cold water over the lid.

Serves 4-6.

Catalan

1 lb (500 g) bottom round, cut
  into cubes
2 small onions, chopped
2 medium tomatoes, chopped
1 sweet green pepper, chopped
1 sweet red pepper, chopped
2 cloves garlic, minced
1 breast of chicken

¼ lb (125 g) ham, chopped
3 medium carrots, sliced
3 teaspoons salt
½ teaspoon black pepper
½ lb (250 g) Italian sausage, cut
  into large cubes
1 lb (500 g) potatoes, sliced
1 lb (500 g) green beans, cut up

1. Put the steak into the pressure cooker and pour in about three cups of water.
2. Add the onions, tomatoes, green and red peppers, garlic and chicken.
3. Cover and pressure cook for 20 minutes. Allow the pressure to reduce gradually.
4. Remove the cover and add the ham, carrots, salt, pepper, sausage, potatoes and beans.
5. Put the cover back on and pressure cook for another ten minutes. Reduce the pressure rapidly by running cold water on the lid or by putting into a sink of cold water.

Serves 6.

Spiced Pot Roast

4 lb (2 kg) boned and rolled beef
  roast
1 teaspoon grated nutmeg
1 teaspoon cinnamon
1 teaspoon grated fresh ginger
2 teaspoons salt
¼ teaspoon black pepper

2 tablespoons vegetable oil
2 medium onions, chopped
1 clove garlic, minced
½ cup brown sugar
¼ cup (65 ml) vinegar
3 bay leaves
1¼ cups (300 ml) beef stock

1. Rub the meat with a mixture of the nutmeg, cinnamon, ginger, salt and pepper. Set aside for 15 minutes.
2. Heat the oil in the open pressure cooker and brown the beef on all sides.
3. Add the onions and garlic and cook until golden brown.
4. Mix together the sugar, vinegar, bay leaves and stock and stir until the sugar is dissolved. Pour into the cooker.
5. Cover and pressure cook for 45 minutes. Allow the pressure to drop gradually.

Serves 8.

Pork with Sauerkraut

2 tablespoons vegetable oil
3 lb (1½ kg) boneless lean pork, in one piece
2 medium onions, chopped
1 clove garlic, minced
1 tablespoon paprika
1 teaspoon salt

½ lb (250 g) Polish sausage, cubed
4 cups sauerkraut
¼ cup (65 g) tomato paste
1 cup (250 ml) beef stock
2 tablespoons flour
⅓ cup (85 ml) water
chopped parsley

1. Heat the oil in the open pressure cooker then brown the meat on all sides.
2. Add the onions, garlic, paprika, salt and Polish sausage. Arrange around the pork.
3. Put the sauerkraut over it all.
4. Mix the tomato paste with the beef stock and pour over the sauerkraut.
5. Cover and pressure cook for 45 minutes. Allow the pressure to reduce gradually. Remove the cover.
6. Put the pork onto a warm serving platter.
7. Blend the flour with the water and stir into the sauerkraut mixture. Cook over a medium heat, stirring constantly, until thickened. Serve over the meat and sprinkle with chopped parsley.

Serves 6-8.

Hungarian Goulash

2 lb (1 kg) boned beef chuck, cubed
½ cup flour
2 tablespoons vegetable oil
1 large onion, chopped
2 cups (500 ml) beef stock
1½ tablespoons paprika
3 teaspoons vinegar

1 tablespoon caraway seeds
1 teaspoon marjoram
2 bay leaves
¼ cup chopped parsley
2 teaspoons capers
salt and pepper
¼ cup (65 ml) dry sherry

1. Dredge the cubed meat in the flour. Shake off any excess.
2. Heat the oil in the open pressure cooker.
3. Sauté the onion in the oil until golden brown.
4. Add the beef and brown well.
5. Pour in the stock and mix well. Add the paprika, vinegar, caraway seeds, marjoram, bay leaves, parsley and capers. Season to taste with salt and pepper.
6. Cover and pressure cook for 15 minutes. Reduce the pressure rapidly by running cold water over the lid.
7. Uncover and add the sherry. Simmer with the lid off for three minutes.

Serves 6.

Stuffed Rolled Roast

4 lb (2 kg) rolled beef roast
1 medium onion, minced
½ sweet red pepper, minced
2 cloves garlic, minced
¼ lb (125 g) ham, minced
2 tablespoons vinegar
1 tablespoon chopped chives
2 tablespoons chopped parsley

1½ teaspoons salt
½ teaspoon black pepper
¼ teaspoon oregano
2 tablespoons vegetable oil
1 cup (250 ml) tomato purée
1 cup chopped black olives
½ sweet red pepper, chopped
1 cup (250 ml) beef stock

1. Unroll the roast and spread it out.
2. Mix together the onion, ½ red pepper, garlic, ham, vinegar, chives, parsley, salt, pepper and oregano.
3. Spread the meat with the mixture then tie up securely.
4. Heat the oil in the open pressure cooker and brown the rolled roast on all sides.
5. Blend together the tomato purée, olives, ½ red pepper and beef stock and pour over the roast.
6. Cover and pressure cook for 40 minutes. Allow the pressure to drop gradually.
7. Uncover and serve the roast with the sauce on top.

Serves 8.

Braised Sweetbreads

1 lb (500 g) sweetbreads
2 tablespoons (40 g) butter
2 slices bacon
3 medium onions, sliced
1 cup chopped celery
4 medium tomatoes, sliced

1¼ cups (300 ml) beef stock
3 tablespoons flour
⅓ cup (85 ml) water
⅔ cup (165 ml) red wine
chopped parsley

1. Put the sweetbreads into the pressure cooker and cover with cold water. Bring to the boil. Remove and dry the sweetbreads. Discard the water.
2. Melt the butter in the cooker. Fry the bacon until crispy. Remove from the cooker and crumble.
3. Sauté the sweetbreads until golden brown. Remove from the cooker.
4. Sauté the onions, celery and tomatoes for two minutes.
5. Pour on the beef stock. Sprinkle on the bacon then put the sweetbreads on top.
6. Cover and pressure cook for six minutes. Reduce the pressure rapidly by running cold water on the lid. Open.
7. Using a slotted spoon, remove the sweetbreads and vegetables from the cooker and put on a warm serving platter.
8. Blend the flour with the water and stir into the liquid in the cooker.
9. Add the red wine and cook over a medium heat, stirring constantly, until thickened. Pour over the sweetbreads.
10. Serve garnished with chopped parsley.

Serves 4.

Braised Liver

¾ lb (375 g) calves' liver
salt and pepper
1½ tablespoons (30 g) butter
¼ lb (125 g) bacon
3 medium onions, sliced
1 clove garlic, minced

3 medium tomatoes, sliced
¼ cup chopped parsley
1 cup sliced celery
1¼ cups (300 ml) beef stock
⅛ teaspoon thyme
chopped chives

1. Season the liver with salt and pepper.
2. Melt the butter in the pressure cooker. Add the bacon and cook until the bacon is crispy. Remove the bacon and crumble it.
3. Brown the liver in the butter and bacon fat on both sides. Remove the liver from the cooker.
4. Sauté the onions, garlic, tomatoes, parsley and celery until the onions are golden brown. Skim off all but one tablespoon of the fat.
5. Pour on the beef stock. Sprinkle on the bacon and thyme. Put the liver on top.
6. Cover and pressure cook for 15 minutes. Reduce the pressure rapidly by running cold water on the lid. Uncover.
7. Serve garnished with chopped chives.

Serves 4.

Pot Roast with Prunes

4 lb (2 kg) boned and rolled beef
   roast
1 tablespoon vegetable oil
½ cup (125 ml) beef stock
2 medium onions, chopped
1 celery stalk, chopped
1 clove garlic, minced

1 bay leaf
½ teaspoon ground nutmeg
1½ teaspoons salt
1½ cups pitted prunes
1½ tablespoons (30 g) butter
1½ tablespoons flour

1. Brown the meat well on all sides in the oil in the open pressure cooker.
2. Add the beef stock, onions, celery, garlic, bay leaf, nutmeg and salt.
3. Cover and pressure cook for 35 minutes. Allow the pressure to reduce gradually.
4. Uncover and put the meat on a warm serving platter.
5. Add the prunes to the sauce in the pressure cooker. Bring to a boil. Reduce heat and simmer for five minutes.
6. Blend together the butter and flour then stir into the prune mixture. Cook until thickened.
7. Pour the prune sauce over the meat, slice and serve immediately.

Serves 8.

Braised Liver with Potatoes

¾ lb (375 g) lamb's liver
salt and pepper
1½ tablespoons (30 g) butter
¼ lb (125 g) bacon
4 medium onions, sliced
1 clove garlic, minced

4 medium potatoes, sliced
⅔ cup (165 ml) chicken stock
½ cup (125 ml) dry white wine
⅛ teaspoon sage
⅓ cup (85 ml) cream
chopped parsley

1. Season the liver with salt and pepper.
2. Melt the butter in the pressure cooker, then cook the bacon until crispy. Remove from the cooker and crumble.
3. Brown the liver on both sides then remove from the cooker.
4. Sauté the onions and garlic until transparent.
5. Add the potato slices and cook on both sides until golden.
6. Remove all but about one tablespoon of fat.
7. Pour on the stock and wine. Sprinkle on the bacon and sage. Put the liver on top.
8. Cover and pressure cook for 15 minutes. Reduce the pressure rapidly by running cold water over the lid. Open.
9. Remove the liver, potatoes and onions from the cooker. Stir in the cream and pour the sauce over the liver and potatoes.
10. Serve garnished with chopped parsley.

Serves 4.

Cream Tripe and Onions

2 lb (1 kg) tripe
4 medium onions, sliced
2 tablespoons (40 g) butter
1¼ cups (300 ml) milk
salt and pepper

3 tablespoons flour
⅓ cup (85 ml) cream
chopped parsley
paprika

1. Cut the tripe into squares and put into the pressure cooker. Pour on enough water to cover and bring to the boil. Remove the tripe and discard the water.
2. Melt the butter in the cooker and sauté the onions until transparent.
3. Add the tripe, milk and salt and pepper to taste.
4. Cover and pressure cook for ten minutes. Reduce the pressure rapidly by running cold water on the lid. Uncover.
5. Blend the flour with the cream and stir into the tripe and onions. Cook over a medium heat, stirring constantly, until thickened.
6. Serve sprinkled with chopped parsley and paprika.

Serves 6.

Tripe with Tomatoes

2 lb (1 kg) tripe
3 medium onions, chopped
1 clove garlic, minced
2 tablespoons (40 g) butter
1¼ cups (300 ml) tomato juice
salt and pepper

1 lb (500 g) tomatoes, chopped
3 tablespoons flour
⅓ cup (85 ml) water
chopped chives
paprika

1. Cut the tripe into squares and put into the pressure cooker. Pour on enough water to cover and bring to a boil. Remove the tripe from the cooker and discard the water.
2. Melt the butter in the cooker and sauté the onions and garlic until golden brown.
3. Add the tomato juice, salt and pepper to taste, chopped tomatoes and the tripe. Mix thoroughly.
4. Cover and pressure cook for ten minutes. Reduce the pressure rapidly by running cold water over the lid. Remove the lid.
5. Blend the flour with the water and stir into the tripe mixture. Cook over a medium heat, stirring constantly, until thickened.
6. Serve sprinkled with chopped chives and paprika.

Serves 6.

Chicken Cacciatore

2 tablespoons (40 g) butter
2 tablespoons olive oil
3 lb (1½ kg) chicken pieces
2 medium onions, chopped
1 clove garlic, minced
¼ lb (125 g) mushrooms, sliced
1 sweet green pepper, chopped

1 lb (500 g) ripe tomatoes, chopped
⅔ cup (165 ml) chicken stock
½ cup (125 ml) dry white wine
½ teaspoon rosemary
salt and pepper
2 tablespoons flour
½ cup (125 ml) cream

1. Heat the butter and oil in the open pressure cooker.
2. Brown the chicken pieces well on all sides. Remove from the cooker.
3. Add the onions and garlic and sauté until golden brown.
4. Add the mushrooms and green pepper and cook for another two minutes, stirring constantly.
5. Return the chicken to the cooker and add the tomatoes, chicken stock, wine, rosemary and salt and pepper to taste.
6. Cover and pressure cook for five minutes. Reduce the pressure rapidly by running cold water over the lid. Remove the lid.
7. Put the chicken on a warm serving platter.
8. Blend the flour with the cream and stir into the sauce. Cook over a medium heat, stirring constantly, until thickened. Pour over the chicken and serve immediately.

Serves 4.

Coq au Vin

2 tablespoons (40 g) butter	3 lb (1½ kg) chicken pieces
¼ lb (125 g) bacon, chopped	1¼ cups (300 ml) white wine
6 small onions, peeled	salt and black pepper
2 cloves garlic, minced	2 tablespoons flour
¼ lb (125 g) button mushrooms	⅓ cup (85 ml) water

1. Melt the butter in the open pressure cooker.
2. Cook the bacon with the onions, garlic and mushrooms until the onions are golden brown.
3. Remove the onions and mushrooms from the cooker.
4. Brown the chicken pieces on all sides.
5. Return the onions and mushrooms to the cooker. Pour on the white wine and season to taste with salt and pepper.
6. Cover and pressure cook for five minutes. Reduce the pressure rapidly by running cold water over the lid. Remove the lid.
7. Put the chicken pieces on a warm serving plate.
8. Blend the flour with the water and stir into the sauce. Cook over a medium heat, stirring constantly, until thickened. Pour over the chicken and serve immediately.

Serves 4.

Ragout of Oxtail

2½ tablespoons (50 g) bacon fat	⅛ teaspoon sage
3 large onions, sliced	⅛ teaspoon thyme
1 clove garlic, minced	¾ lb (375 g) carrots, sliced
2 oxtails, jointed	2½ tablespoons flour
1¾ cups (435 ml) beef stock	½ cup (125 ml) red wine
salt and pepper	

1. Heat the bacon fat in the open pressure cooker.
2. Sauté the onions and garlic until golden brown. Remove the onions from the cooker and keep warm.
3. Brown the oxtails in the open pressure cooker.
4. Add the beef stock, salt and pepper to taste, sage and thyme.
5. Cover and pressure cook for ten minutes. Reduce the pressure rapidly by running cold water over the lid.
6. Remove the lid and add the onions and carrots. Re-cover and pressure cook for five minutes. Reduce the pressure rapidly again.
7. Blend the flour with the wine and stir into ragout. Cook over a medium heat, stirring constantly, until thickened.

Serves 4.

Chicken Chausseur

3 lb (1½ kg) chicken pieces
2 tablespoons (40 g) butter
2 tablespoons olive oil
2 small onions, chopped
1 clove garlic, minced
¼ lb (125 g) fresh mushrooms, sliced

1 lb (500 g) tomatoes, chopped
⅔ cup (165 ml) chicken stock
½ cup (125 ml) dry white wine
1 tablespoon chopped tarragon
1 tablespoon chopped parsley
2 tablespoons flour
½ cup (125 ml) cream

1. Brown the chicken pieces on all sides in the butter and olive oil in the open pressure cooker. Remove the chicken from the cooker.
2. Sauté the onions and garlic until golden brown.
3. Add the mushrooms and cook for one minute.
4. Put the chicken back in the cooker and add the tomatoes, chicken stock, wine, tarragon and parsley.
5. Cover and pressure cook for five minutes. Reduce the pressure rapidly by running cold water over the lid.
6. Take off the lid and remove the chicken to a warm serving plate.
7. Blend the flour with the cream and stir into the sauce. Cook over a medium heat, stirring constantly, until thickened. Pour over the chicken and serve.

Serves 4.

Beef Olives

Filling:
2 teaspoons grated lemon rind
¼ cup (65 ml) lemon juice
2 cups soft bread crumbs
2 tablespoons chopped parsley
1 tablespoon chopped chives
1 tablespoon chopped fresh basil
3 tablespoons (60 g) butter
salt and black pepper
1 large egg

1½ lb (750 g) bottom round, cut
  into four thin slices
2½ tablespoons (50 g) bacon fat
1⅔ cups (415 ml) beef stock
1 bay leaf
10 black peppercorns
salt
½ lb (250 g) shelled fresh peas
2 tablespoons flour
⅓ cup (85 ml) water

1. Mix together the lemon rind, lemon juice, bread crumbs, parsley, chives, basil, butter, salt and pepper to taste and the egg. Beat until thoroughly combined.
2. Pound the meat until thin. If the pieces are too big, cut them in half.
3. Spread the filling on each piece of meat. Roll up and tie securely.
4. Heat the bacon fat in the open pressure cooker. Brown the beef olives on all sides.
5. Pour in the beef stock and add the bay leaf, peppercorns and salt to taste.
6. Cover and pressure cook for 15 minutes. Reduce the pressure rapidly by running cold water over the lid. Remove the lid.
7. Add the peas, cover and pressure cook for three minutes. Again reduce the pressure. Open the cooker.
8. Put the beef olives and peas onto a warm serving platter.
9. Blend the flour with the water and stir into the liquid in the cooker. Cook over a medium heat, stirring constantly, until thickened. Remove the bay leaf and the peppercorns. Pour the sauce over the beef olives and serve immediately.

Serves 4.

Moroccan Lamb

1½ lb (750 g) leg lamb, cut into cubes
½ teaspoon ground ginger
½ teaspoon powdered saffron
½ teaspoon grated fresh ginger
3 teaspoons grated lemon rind

1 teaspoon grated orange rind
salt and black pepper
3 medium onions, sliced
2½ tablespoons (50 g) butter
1¼ cups (300 ml) chicken stock

1. Mix together the ginger, saffron, grated ginger, lemon and orange rind and salt and pepper to taste. Rub into the lamb cubes.
2. Sauté the onions in the butter in the open pressure cooker until golden brown.
3. Add the meat and brown well.
4. Pour on the chicken stock and mix thoroughly.
5. Cover and pressure cook for ten minutes. Reduce the pressure rapidly by running cold water over the lid. Delicious served with hot buttered noodles.

Serves 4.

Blanquette of Veal

2 medium onions, chopped
½ clove garlic, minced
3 tablespoons (60 g) butter
1½ lb (750 g) stewing veal
1 bouquet garni
1¼ cups (300 ml) chicken stock

salt and black pepper
2 tablespoons flour
⅔ cup (165 ml) cream
2 egg yolks
1½ tablespoons lemon juice

1. Sauté the onions and garlic in the butter until golden brown.
2. Add the veal and brown well.
3. Stir in the bouquet garni, chicken stock and salt and pepper to taste.
4. Cover and pressure cook for ten minutes. Reduce the pressure rapidly by running cold water over the lid. Remove the lid.
5. Beat the flour with the cream, egg yolks and lemon juice. Stir into the stew and heat gently for two minutes, stirring constantly.

Serves 4.

Savory Ground Beef

3 tablespoons (60 g) bacon fat
2 medium onions, chopped
3 medium tomatoes, sliced
2 medium carrots, diced
1 turnip, diced
1 clove garlic, minced

1¼ cups (300 ml) beef stock
1 lb (500 g) ground beef
salt and black pepper
2 tablespoons flour
⅓ cup (85 ml) water
hot cooked rice or noodles

1. Heat the bacon fat in the open pressure cooker then add the onions, tomatoes, carrots, turnip and garlic. Sauté for three minutes, stirring constantly.
2. Add the beef stock and mix well.
3. Add the meat and cook over a medium heat for 10 minutes stirring constantly to break up the meat.
4. Season to taste with salt and pepper.
5. Cover and pressure cook for five minutes. Reduce the pressure rapidly by running cold water over the lid. Remove the lid.
6. Blend the flour with the water then stir into the meat mixture. Cook over a medium heat, stirring constantly, until thickened.
7. Serve with rice or noodles.

Serves 3-4.

Lamb with Saffron

2 lb (1 kg) neck chops
1½ lb (750 g) potatoes, peeled and thickly sliced
6 medium onions, thickly sliced
2 medium carrots, sliced

⅔ cup (165 ml) water
½ cup (125 ml) dry white wine
salt and black pepper
⅔ cup (165 ml) cream
½ teaspoon powdered saffron

1. Put the chops on the bottom of the pressure cooker with the potatoes, onions and carrots on top.
2. Pour on the water and wine and season with salt and black pepper.
3. Cover and pressure cook for ten minutes. Reduce the pressure rapidly by running cold water over the lid. Remove the lid.
4. Put the vegetables and chops on a warm serving platter.
5. Take ⅔ cup (165 ml) of the stock in the pressure cooker and mix it with the cream and saffron in a small saucepan. Heat through and pour over the chops and vegetables.

Serves 4.

Veal Marengo

1½ lb (750 g) stewing veal
⅓ cup flour
2 teaspoons salt
1 teaspoon black pepper
¼ cup (65 ml) olive oil
2 medium onions, sliced
1 clove garlic, minced
1 cup (250 ml) dry white wine
1 cup (250 ml) chicken stock
2 tablespoons tomato paste

½ teaspoon grated orange rind
¼ teaspoon tarragon
¼ teaspoon thyme
¼ lb (125 g) fresh mushrooms, sliced
2 tablespoons flour
⅓ cup (85 ml) water
salt and pepper
hot cooked rice
chopped parsley

1. Cut the veal into small cubes. Coat with a mixture of the flour, salt and pepper. Shake off any excess flour.
2. Heat the oil in the open pressure cooker and sauté the onions and garlic until golden brown.
3. Add the meat and brown well.
4. Mix together the wine, chicken stock, tomato paste, orange rind, tarragon and thyme. Pour over the veal and mix well.
5. Stir in the mushrooms.
6. Cover and pressure cook for 15 minutes. Reduce the pressure rapidly by running cold water over the lid. Remove the lid.
7. Blend together the flour and water and stir into the veal. Cook over a medium heat, stirring constantly, until thickened.
8. Season to taste with salt and pepper.
9. Serve over hot cooked rice and sprinkle with chopped parsley.

Serves 4.

Hungarian Chicken

4 lb (2 kg) chicken pieces
¾ cup flour
1 tablespoon paprika
1½ teaspoons salt
¼ teaspoon cayenne pepper
½ teaspoon black pepper
¼ teaspoon ginger
¼ teaspoon thyme

¼ cup (65 g) butter
2 cups (500 ml) chicken stock
1½ tablespoons Worcestershire sauce
¼ cup (65 g) chili sauce
2 cloves garlic, minced
2 cups (500 g) sour cream
½ cup (125 ml) dry sherry

1. Dampen the chicken with water.
2. Mix together the flour, paprika, salt, cayenne and black pepper, ginger and thyme.
3. Coat the chicken with the flour mixture shaking off any excess.
4. Melt the butter in the open pressure cooker and brown the chicken pieces thoroughly.
5. Mix together the stock, Worcestershire sauce, chili sauce and garlic and pour over the chicken.
6. Cover and pressure cook for 20 minutes. Allow the pressure to reduce gradually for ten minutes, then run cold water over the lid to bring it down rapidly.
7. Remove the cover and add the sour cream and sherry. Heat through and serve.

Serves 6.

Chicken with Cumquats

3 lb (1½ kg) chicken pieces
1 teaspoon salt
½ teaspoon freshly ground black pepper
½ cup (125 ml) orange juice

2 tablespoons lemon juice
½ cup (125 ml) honey
1 teaspoon minced red chilies
10 preserved cumquats
cooked white rice

1. Rub the chicken pieces with salt and pepper.
2. Combine the orange juice, lemon juice, honey and red chilies in a small saucepan and stir over a low heat until the honey is melted.
3. Put the chicken pieces into the pressure cooker and pour the orange and honey sauce over it.
4. Cover and pressure cook for ten minutes. Reduce the pressure rapidly by running cold water over the lid.
5. Uncover and add the cumquats. Heat gently until the cumquats are warm through. Serve with hot cooked rice.

Serves 4.

Steak and Kidney

1½ lb (750 g) boned beef chuck   salt and black pepper
½ lb (250 g) kidneys   1¾ cups (435 ml) beef stock
2 tablespoons vegetable oil   bouquet garni
2 medium onions, chopped   2 tablespoons flour
1½ tablespoons tomato paste   ⅓ cup (85 ml) water

1. Cut the chuck steak into cubes removing any fat. Dice the kidneys.
2. Heat the oil in an open pressure and sauté the onions until transparent.
3. Add the steak and kidneys and brown well.
4. Stir in the tomato paste, salt and pepper to taste, beef stock and bouquet garni.
5. Cover and pressure cook for 15-20 minutes. Reduce the pressure rapidly by running cold water over the lid.
6. Blend together the flour and water and stir into the steak and kidney. Stir over a medium heat until thickened. Remove the bouquet garni before serving.

Serves 6.

Corned Beef and Vegetables

3 lb (1½ kg) corned brisket of beef   ½ lb (250 g) turnips
½ lb (250 g) carrots, thickly sliced   ½ teaspoon black pepper
3 medium onions, halved   mustard
10 cloves   horseradish sauce

1. Put the brisket in the pressure cooker and add enough cold water to cover. Slowly bring to a boil. Remove from the heat and allow the meat to stay in the water for about five minutes. Pour out the water.
2. Pour in enough fresh water to half-fill the cooker.
3. Put in a few carrot slices, one onion and the cloves.
4. Cover and pressure cook for seven minutes. Reduce the pressure rapidly by running cold water over the lid. Open.
5. Add the rest of the carrots and onions and put in the turnips and black pepper.
6. Cover and pressure cook for five minutes. Again reduce the pressure rapidly.
7. Remove the brisket and vegetables from the water and serve with mustard and horseradish sauce.

Serves 6.

Boiled Lamb with Sauce

½ large leg of lamb
½ lb (250 g) carrots, thickly sliced
3 medium onions, thickly sliced
10 peppercorns
6 whole cloves
½ lb (250 g) turnips, thickly sliced
salt and pepper

Sauce:
2 tablespoons (40 g) butter
2 tablespoons flour
1¼ cups (300 ml) stock
½ cup (125 ml) cream
2 tablespoons capers
1 teaspoon lemon juice
chopped chives

1. Put the lamb in the pressure cooker with enough cold water to half-fill the cooker. Add a few slices of carrots, one onion, the peppercorns and cloves.
2. Cover and pressure cook for ten minutes. Reduce the pressure rapidly by running cold water over the lid.
3. Remove the lid and add the rest of the carrots, onions and turnips. Season to taste with salt and pepper.
4. Cover and pressure cook for five minutes. Again, reduce the pressure rapidly and uncover.
5. Melt the butter in a small saucepan. Remove from the heat and stir in the flour. Return to the heat and cook over a low heat for one minute.
6. Take 1¼ cups of stock from the cooker and slowly add the butter and flour mixture, stirring constantly, until thick.
7. Add the cream, capers and lemon juice. Heat through and serve over the lamb and vegetables. Sprinkle with chives.

Serves 4.

Chicken Curry

2 small onions, chopped
1 clove garlic, minced
1 large cooking apple, chopped
1 tablespoon curry powder (or to taste)
3 tablespoons (60 g) butter
1⅔ cups (415 ml) chicken stock
¼ cup raisins

2 tablespoons flaked coconut
2 tablespoons chutney
salt and black pepper
½ teaspoon brown sugar
¼ cup (65 ml) lemon juice
1½ lb (750 g) raw white chicken meat, diced
hot white rice

1. Cook the onions, garlic, apple and curry powder in the butter in the open pressure cooker for three minutes, stirring constantly.
2. Add the chicken stock, raisins, coconut, chutney, salt and pepper to taste, sugar, lemon juice and chicken. Mix well.
3. Cover and pressure cook for eight minutes. Reduce the pressure rapidly by running cold water over the lid of the cooker. Remove the lid and mix again.
4. Serve with hot rice.

Serves 4-6.

Herbed Chicken

3 lb (1½ kg) chicken pieces
3 tablespoons (60 g) butter
2 medium onions, sliced
3 medium tomatoes, sliced
¼ cup chopped parsley
1¼ cups (300 ml) chicken stock
salt and black pepper

2 tablespoons chopped fresh chives
2 tablespoons chopped fresh basil
1 tablespoon fresh rosemary
1 tablespoon chopped fresh sage
hot cooked brown rice
chopped parsley

1. Brown the chicken pieces in the butter in the open pressure cooker. Remove the chicken.
2. Sauté the onions until golden brown.
3. Add the tomatoes, sprinkle on the parsley and pour on the chicken stock. Season to taste with salt and pepper.
4. Put the chicken on top of the onions and tomatoes.
5. Sprinkle the herbs over the chicken.
6. Cover and pressure cook for five minutes. Reduce the pressure rapidly by running cold water over the lid.
7. Serve with brown rice and garnish with chopped parsley.

Serves 4-6.

Creamed Ground Beef

2 medium onions, minced
1 clove garlic, minced
2 tablespoons (40 g) bacon fat
2 medium potatoes, peeled and diced
1¼ cups (300 ml) beef stock

1½ teaspoons grated lemon rind
1 lb (500 g) ground beef
salt and black pepper
2 tablespoons flour
½ cup (125 ml) cream
hot cooked noodles

1. Sauté the onions and garlic in the bacon fat in the open pressure cooker until transparent.
2. Add the potatoes and cook until golden brown.
3. Add the beef stock and lemon rind and bring to a boil.
4. Stir in the beef, mixing well to keep the beef broken up.
5. Season to taste with salt and pepper.
6. Cover and pressure cook for five minutes. Reduce the pressure rapidly by running cold water over the lid. Remove the cover.
7. Mix the flour with the cream. Stir into the beef mixture and cook over a low heat until thickened.
8. Serve with hot cooked noodles.

Serves 4.

Chili Con Carne

2 medium onions, chopped
2 cloves garlic, minced
2 tablespoons (40 g) bacon fat
1 sweet green pepper, chopped
1 cup chopped celery
3 medium tomatoes, chopped
1 teaspoon chili powder or to taste

1¼ cups (300 ml) beef stock
1 lb (500 g) ground beef
salt and pepper
2 cups canned kidney beans
2 tablespoons flour
¼ cup (65 ml) cold water
cooked white rice

1. Sauté the onions and garlic in the bacon fat until golden brown.
2. Add the pepper, celery, tomatoes and chili powder and cook over a medium heat for two minutes.
3. Add the beef stock and bring to a boil.
4. Add the ground beef and stir until the beef is broken up.
5. Season to taste with salt and pepper.
6. Add the drained kidney beans, cover and pressure cook for five minutes. Reduce the pressure rapidly by running cold water over the lid. Remove the cover.
7. Mix the flour with the cold water. Stir into the chili con carne and cook, stirring constantly, until thickened.
8. Serve with cooked white rice.

Serves 4.

Pot Roast

4 lb (2 kg) boned and rolled beef
   roast
2 tablespoons vegetable oil
1 medium onion, chopped
1 clove garlic, minced

1 teaspoon salt
½ teaspoon black pepper
½ cup (125 ml) water
cornstarch

1. Brown the meat in the oil in the open pressure cooker. Remove and keep warm.
2. Sauté the onion and garlic in the pressure cooker until golden brown.
3. Return the meat to the cooker. Season with salt and pepper.
4. Add the water and pressure cook for about 40 minutes.
5. Reduce the pressure and transfer the meat to a serving platter.
6. Add a little cornstarch to the liquid in the cooker to make a gravy. Pour over the meat, slice and serve.

Serves 8.

Lamb's Tongues with Redcurrant Sauce

1½ lb (750 g) lambs' tongues
2 medium carrots, peeled and
   cut into thick slices
4 small onions, peeled
2 medium turnips, peeled and
   cut into thick slices
water
freshly ground black pepper

Redcurrant Sauce:
1 tablespoon cornstarch
1¼ cups (300 ml) stock
1 cup (250 ml) Madeira wine
¼ cup redcurrant jam
1 teaspoon grated orange rind
½ teaspoon grated lemon rind

1. Put the lambs' tongues into the pressure cooker with the carrots, onions and turnips.
2. Add enough water to half-fill the cooker. Season to taste with black pepper.
3. Cover and pressure cook for 20 minutes. Reduce the pressure rapidly by running cold water over the lid. Remove the cover and put the lambs' tongues and vegetables on a warm serving platter. Strain the stock.
4. Mix the cornstarch with a little of the stock in a saucepan.
5. Add the rest of the stock, the Madeira wine, jam, orange and lemon rinds. Heat gently, stirring constantly, until the sauce is thickened and clear.
6. Pour over the tongues and vegetables and serve immediately.

Serves 4.

Sauces

Tomato Sauce (1)

¼ cup (65 ml) olive oil
2 medium onions, chopped
2 cloves garlic, minced
1 lb (500 g) ground beef
2 lb (1 kg) canned tomatoes
¾ cup (185 g) tomato paste
1 bay leaf

¼ cup (65 ml) water
½ cup chopped celery
¼ cup chopped parsley
3 teaspoons salt
1 teaspoon sugar
¼ teaspoon black pepper
½ teaspoon basil

1. Heat the oil in the open pressure cooker and sauté the onions and garlic for five minutes.
2. Add the meat and cook until it is brown, breaking the meat up as it cooks.
3. Add the remaining ingredients and mix thoroughly.
4. Cover and pressure cook for 15 minutes. Allow the pressure to drop gradually.

Makes about 4-5 cups.

Mint Sauce

1 cup fresh mint leaves
1 cup (250 ml) vinegar
½ cup sugar
½ cup (125 ml) water
¼ teaspoon salt

1. Wash and dry the mint leaves thoroughly.
2. Put into the pressure cooker with the vinegar, sugar, water and salt.
3. Cover and pressure cook for five minutes. Bring the pressure down rapidly by running cold water on the lid of the cooker.
4. Put into an electric blender and whirl until well-minced, or pour through a strainer if a clear sauce is wanted.

Makes about 2 cups.

Cumberland Sauce

3 large oranges
1 large lemon
1¼ cups (300 ml) chicken stock
3 teaspoons cornstarch

½ teaspoon hot English mustard
⅓ cup (85 ml) port
½ cup redcurrant jam
salt and white pepper

1. Cut the rind from the oranges and lemons making sure not to cut any of the pith with it. Cut the rind into thin strips.
2. Put the rind and the chicken stock into the pressure cooker and pressure cook for five minutes. Allow the pressure to reduce gradually.
3. Meanwhile squeeze the juice from the oranges and lemon.
4. Blend the cornstarch with a little of the juice.
5. Heat together the juices, mustard, port, jam, salt and pepper to taste and the liquid from the cooker.
6. Add the cornstarch mixture, stirring constantly. Cook over a low heat until thickened.

Makes about 3 cups.

Mexican Sauce

1½ tablespoons (30 g) butter
2 slices bacon, diced
1 medium onion, chopped
1 clove garlic, minced
3 medium tomatoes, sliced
1 sweet green pepper, chopped

1¼ cups (300 ml) beef stock
¼ teaspoon chili powder
salt and pepper
2 tablespoons flour
¼ cup (65 ml) dry sherry

1. Heat the butter in the pressure cooker. Add the bacon and cook until crispy.
2. Sauté the onion and garlic until transparent.
3. Add the tomatoes, pepper, beef stock, chili powder and salt and pepper to taste.
4. Cover and pressure cook for seven minutes. Allow the pressure to reduce gradually. Remove the lid.
5. Pour into an electric blender and whirl until smooth. Return to the cooker.
6. Blend the flour with the sherry and stir into the sauce. Cook over a medium heat, stirring constantly, until thickened.

Makes about 3 cups.

Bolognese Sauce

2 tablespoons olive oil
1 medium onion, chopped
2 cloves garlic, minced
1 small carrot, chopped
4 medium tomatoes, chopped
1 sweet green pepper, chopped

¼ lb (125 g) fresh mushrooms, sliced
⅔ cup (165 ml) tomato juice
½ cup (125 ml) red wine
½ lb (250 g) ground beef
salt and pepper

1. Heat the olive oil in the pressure cooker and sauté the onion and garlic until golden brown.
2. Add the carrot, tomatoes, green pepper and mushrooms and cook over a medium heat for two minutes.
3. Mix in the tomato juice, red wine, ground beef and salt and pepper to taste. Bring to a boil.
4. Cover and pressure cook for five minutes. Reduce the pressure rapidly by running cold water over the lid. Remove the pressure.
5. Simmer the sauce, uncovered, for about seven minutes to reduce the liquid.

Makes about 4-5 cups.

Tomato Sauce (2)

1½ lb (750 g) ripe tomatoes, chopped
2 small onions, chopped
1 small cooking apple
1 clove garlic, minced
2 slices bacon, diced

2 tablespoons (40 g) butter
1¼ cups (300 ml) water
½ teaspoon sugar
salt and black pepper
1 tablespoon cornstarch

1. Put all the ingredients except the cornstarch into the pressure cooker. Mix well.
2. Cover and pressure cook for five minutes.
3. Pour all into an electric blender and whirl until almost smooth. Pour back into the cooker.
4. Mix the cornstarch with a little water, then stir into the sauce. Cook over a medium heat, stirring constantly, until thickened.

Makes about 4-5 cups.

Rice and Pasta

Rice

1 cup long grain rice
2½ cups (625 ml) water
½ teaspoon salt

1. Put the water and salt into the pressure cooker and bring to a boil.
2. Add the rice, stir well.
3. Cover and pressure cook for five minutes. Reduce the pressure quickly by running cold water over the lid.
4. Remove the cover and strain and rinse the rice.

Serves 4.

Rice Curry

1½ tablespoons (30 g) bacon fat	¼ cup raisins
2 medium onions, chopped	1 tablespoon flaked coconut
1 clove garlic, minced	1 cooking apple, chopped
1 cup long grain rice	½ cup fresh peas
2½ cups (625 ml) chicken stock	salt and black pepper

1. Heat the bacon fat in the open pressure cooker and sauté the onions and garlic until golden brown.
2. Add the rice and cook until golden, stirring constantly.
3. Pour on the chicken stock and stir in the raisins, coconut, apple, peas and salt and pepper to taste.
4. Cover and pressure cook for five minutes. Reduce the pressure rapidly by running cold water over the lid. Uncover and stir. Drain off any excess liquid.

Serves 4.

Rice with Lemon

2½ cups (625 ml) water
½ teaspoon salt
2 tablespoons lemon juice
1 teaspoon grated lemon rind
½ teaspoon nutmeg
1 cup long grain rice

1. Put the water, salt, lemon juice, grated lemon rind and nutmeg into the pressure cooker and bring to a boil.
2. Add the rice and mix well.
3. Cover and pressure cook for five minutes. Reduce the pressure rapidly by running cold water over the lid.
4. Remove the cover and strain the rice.

Serves 4.

Savory Rice

1 tablespoon (20 g) butter
1 medium onion, chopped
1 clove garlic, minced
½ sweet green pepper, chopped
2 medium tomatoes, chopped

2½ cups (625 ml) beef stock
2 tablespoons chopped parsley
salt and pepper
1 cup long grain rice

1. Melt the butter in the open pressure cooker and sauté the onion and garlic until golden brown.
2. Add the pepper and tomatoes and cook over a medium heat, stirring constantly, for one minute.
3. Add the beef stock, parsley and salt and pepper to taste. Mix well and bring to a boil.
4. Stir in the rice, cover and pressure cook for five minutes. Reduce the pressure rapidly by running cold water over the lid. Uncover and stir.

Serves 4.

Golden Rice

2 small onions, chopped
1 clove garlic, minced
2 tablespoons (40 g) butter
1 teaspoon salt
2½ cups (625 ml) saffron
   flavored stock
1¼ cups long grain rice

1. Sauté the onions and garlic in the butter in the open pressure cooker until golden brown.
2. Add the salt and stock and bring to a boil.
3. Stir in the rice, cover and pressure cook for five minutes. Reduce the pressure quickly by running cold water over the lid. Uncover and stir.

Serves 4.

Rice Supreme

1 medium onion, chopped	2 medium tomatoes, chopped
1 clove garlic, minced	1 cup chopped celery
½ sweet green pepper, chopped	½ lb (250 g) chicken livers, diced
2 tablespoons (40 g) butter	salt and black pepper
1 tablespoon olive oil	2½ cups (625 ml) chicken stock
¼ lb (125 g) fresh mushrooms, chopped	1¼ cups long grain rice

1. Sauté the onion, garlic and green pepper in the butter and oil in the open pressure cooker until the onions are golden brown.
2. Add the mushrooms, tomatoes, celery, chicken livers and salt and pepper to taste. Cook over a medium heat, stirring constantly, for two minutes.
3. Stir in the chicken stock and bring to a boil.
4. Add the rice, stir and cover. Pressure cook for five minutes. Reduce the pressure rapidly by running cold water over the lid. Uncover and stir well.

Serves 4.

Macaroni with Onion

4 cups (1 liter) water	2 medium onions, chopped
1 teaspoon salt	2 cloves garlic, minced
½ lb (250 g) macaroni	2 tablespoons chopped parsley
2 tablespoons (40 g) butter	½ lb (250 g) Mozzarella cheese
2 tablespoons olive oil	

1. Put the water in the pressure cooker with the salt and bring to a boil.
2. Add the macaroni and stir well.
3. Cover and pressure cook for five minutes. Reduce the pressure rapidly by running cold water over the lid. Uncover and drain the macaroni in a colander. Keep warm.
4. Melt the butter in the pressure cooker. Add the oil and heat.
5. Sauté the onions and garlic until the onions are golden brown.
6. Add the parsley and cook for ½ minute.
7. Stir in the drained macaroni ensuring that it is well-coated. Pour into a shallow casserole dish.
8. Slice the Mozzarella cheese and arrange the cheese on top.
9. Put into a 350°F (180°C) oven and cook until the cheese is golden brown.

Serves 4.

Spaghetti

4 cups (1 liter) water
1 teaspoon salt
½ lb (250 g) spaghetti
butter
grated Parmesan cheese
chopped parsley

1. Pour the water into the pressure cooker and bring to a boil.
2. Add the salt and spaghetti, stir and cover. Pressure cook for five minutes (vermicelli takes a shorter time). Reduce the pressure rapidly by running cold water over the lid.
3. Uncover and drain the spaghetti in a colander.
4. Melt some butter in the pressure cooker and stir the spaghetti around in it.
5. Serve sprinkled with Parmesan cheese and chopped parsley.

Serves 4.

Macaroni

4 cups (1 liter) water
1 teaspoon salt
½ lb (250.g) macaroni
¼ cup (65 g) butter
2 tablespoons chopped chives
freshly ground black pepper

1. Pour the water into the pressure cooker with the salt and bring to a boil.
2. Add the macaroni, stir and cover. Pressure cook for five minutes. Reduce the pressure quickly by running cold water over the lid. Uncover.
3. Drain the macaroni in a colander.
4. Melt the butter in the pressure cooker and toss in the chives.
5. Stir in the macaroni and heat through.
6. Pour into a serving dish with all the butter and chives poured over the macaroni. Grind lots of black pepper on top.

Serves 4.

Macaroni and Cheese

2½ cups (625 ml) water
1 teaspoon salt
½ lb (250 g) macaroni
2 tablespoons (40 g) butter
3 tablespoons Parmesan cheese
2 tablespoons chopped parsley

Cheese Sauce:
2 tablespoons (40 g) butter
2 tablespoons flour
salt and pepper
2 cups (500 ml) milk
1 cup grated Cheddar cheese

1. Pour the water into the pressure cooker with the salt and bring to a boil.
2. Add the macaroni and stir.
3. Cover and pressure cook for five minutes. Reduce the pressure rapidly by running cold water over the lid. Uncover.
4. Drain the macaroni in a colander.
5. Melt the butter in the pressure cooker, then stir in macaroni ensuring that the macaroni is well-coated.
6. Add the Parmesan cheese and parsley and mix well. Put into a casserole dish and keep warm.
7. Melt the butter in a small saucepan. Remove from the heat and stir in the flour. Return to the heat and cook for one minute. Season to taste with salt and pepper.
8. Slowly add the milk, stirring constantly. Cook until thickened.
9. Add the cheese and cook until the cheese is melted.
10. Pour over the macaroni. If necessary, heat through in the oven.

Serves 4.

Soups

Fruit Soup

4 cups (1 liter) water
3 cooking apples, peeled and
   diced
½ lb (250 g) rhubarb, chopped
½ lb (250 g) cherries, stoned
½ lb (250 g) plums, stoned
¼ lb (125 g) peaches, stoned

3 tablespoons lemon juice
2 teaspoons grated lemon rind
salt and pepper
sugar
⅛ teaspoon cinnamon
1½ cups (375 g) sour cream
sliced strawberries

1. Put the water into the pressure cooker with the apples, rhubarb, cherries, plums, peaches, lemon juice and lemon rind.
2. Cover and pressure cook for three minutes.
3. Add salt and pepper and sugar to taste and the cinnamon.
4. Pour the mixture into an electric blender and whirl until puréed, or press the fruit through a sieve.
5. Pour into a serving bowl and add the sour cream. Stir until thoroughly blended. Serve cold garnished with strawberries.

Serves 6.

Almond Soup

½ lb (250 g) ground almonds
1 medium onion, chopped
2 tomatoes, chopped
2 cups (500 ml) chicken stock

salt
2 cups (500 ml) cream
1½ tablespoons (30 g) butter
cooked crumbled bacon

1. Put the almonds into the pressure cooker with the onion, tomatoes, chicken stock and salt to taste.
2. Cover and pressure cook for seven minutes. Allow pressure to drop, then remove the lid.
3. Pour into an electric blender and whirl until smooth. Return to the cooker.
4. Add the cream and butter and heat, stirring constantly, until the butter melts.
5. Serve hot garnished with crumbled bacon.

Serves 4.

Mulligatawny Soup

2 small onions, chopped
1 medium carrot, chopped
1 clove garlic, minced
1 cooking apple, peeled and diced
3 tablespoons (60 g) butter
1 tablespoon curry powder

½ teaspoon powdered mustard
1 cup cooked diced meat (chicken or lamb)
6 cups (1½ liters) chicken stock
salt and black pepper
2 tablespoons lemon juice
chopped parsley

1. Sauté the onions, carrot, garlic and apple in the butter in the open pressure cooker for three minutes, stirring frequently.
2. Add the curry powder and mustard and mix well.
3. Add the meat, chicken stock and salt and pepper to taste.
4. Cover and pressure cook for six minutes. Allow the pressure to drop, then remove the cover.
5. Stir in the lemon juice and serve hot garnished with chopped parsley.

Serves 6.

Minestrone

½ cup dried haricot beans
boiling beef stock
2 cloves garlic, minced
2 medium onions, chopped
3 medium tomatoes, chopped
1 medium carrot, chopped
1 stalk celery, chopped

¼ lb (125 g) bacon, chopped
2 cups shredded cabbage
2 tablespoons chopped parsley
salt and freshly ground black
  pepper
¼ cup noodles
Parmesan cheese

1. Pour on enough boiling stock to cover the beans. Set aside to soak for one hour. (Or soak overnight in cold water.)
2. Pour the beans with the stock into the pressure cooker. Make up to 6 cups (1½ liters) with more stock.
3. Cover and pressure cook for 15 minutes. Allow the pressure to reduce, then remove the cover.
4. Add the garlic, onions, tomatoes, carrot, celery, bacon, cabbage, parsley, salt and pepper to taste and noodles. Mix well, cover and pressure cook for eight minutes. Allow the pressure to drop, then remove the cover.
5. Serve hot with Parmesan cheese sprinkled on top.

Serves 6.

Cabbage Soup

¼ lb (125 g) bacon
2 small onions, chopped
2 medium carrots, chopped
½ small cabbage, shredded
6 cups (1½ liters) chicken stock
salt and white pepper

2 tablespoons flour
½ cup (125 ml) milk
1 cup (250 ml) cream
2 tablespoons (40 g) butter
chopped chives

1. Dice the bacon and cook in the open pressure cooker until the fat begins to melt.
2. Add the onions and carrots and cook over a medium heat for two minutes.
3. Add the cabbage, chicken stock and salt and pepper to taste.
4. Cover and pressure cook for two minutes. Allow pressure to reduce, then open.
5. Blend the flour with the milk, then stir into the soup. Bring to a boil, stirring constantly. Reduce heat and simmer for two minutes. Remove from the heat.
6. Stir in the cream and butter until the butter melts.
7. Serve hot garnished with chopped chives.

Serves 6-8.

Fish Soup

2 small onions, chopped	6 cups (1½ liters) water
2 small carrots, chopped	salt and white pepper
1 stalk celery, chopped	2 tablespoons flour
1½ tablespoons (30 g) butter	½ cup (125 ml) milk
1 lb (500 g) white fish fillets, diced	1 cup (250 ml) cream
	chopped parsley

1. Sauté the onions, carrots, and celery in the butter in the open pressure cooker until the onions are transparent.
2. Add the fish, water and salt and pepper to taste.
3. Cover and pressure cook for two minutes. Let the pressure drop and remove the cover.
4. Blend the flour with the milk and stir into the soup. Bring to a boil, stirring constantly. Reduce the heat and simmer for two minutes. Remove from heat.
5. Stir in the cream.
6. Serve hot garnished with chopped parsley.

Serves 6-8.

Split Pea Soup

¼ lb (125 g) split peas	salt
water	freshly ground black pepper
1 cup chopped onions	1 teaspoon sugar
½ cup chopped carrots	1 tablespoon chopped mint
½ cup chopped celery	1 cup chopped ham

1. Put the peas in a bowl and cover with cold water. Set aside and allow to soak overnight.
2. Transfer the peas with the soaking water into the pressure cooker. (There should be about 4 cups of peas and water. If not, add more water.)
3. Add the onions, carrots, celery, salt and pepper to taste, sugar and mint. Cover and pressure cook for ten minutes. Allow pressure to drop, then uncover.
4. Put the pea soup into an electric blender and whirl until smooth, or press through a strainer. Return to the cooker. If the soup is too thick, add a little water.
5. Add the ham and heat through. Serve hot.

Serves 4.

Red Lentil Soup

1½ cups chopped celery
¼ lb (125 g) potatoes, peeled and diced
¼ lb (125 g) red lentils
salt

freshly ground black pepper
¼ teaspoon sage
1 bay leaf
4 cups (1 liter) chicken stock
1 cup (250 ml) cream

1. Put the celery, potatoes, lentils, salt and pepper to taste, sage, bay leaf and chicken stock in the pressure cooker. Mix well.
2. Cover and pressure cook for 15 minutes. Allow pressure to drop and uncover.
3. Remove the bay leaf and purée the mixture in an electric blender or press through a strainer. Return to the cooker and heat through.
4. Stir in the cream. Do not boil. Serve hot.

Serves 6.

Cream of Tomato Soup

1 large onion
1 clove garlic
4 tablespoons (80 g) butter
1 cup chopped celery
2 lb (1 kg) tomatoes, chopped
2½ cups (625 ml) chicken stock
salt and freshly ground black pepper

2 tablespoons (40 g) butter
2 tablespoons flour
1½ cups (375 ml) milk
1 cup (250 ml) cream
chopped parsley
paprika

1. Peel and chop the onion and sauté with the garlic in the butter until the onion is transparent.
2. Add the celery and tomatoes and cook over a low heat for three minutes, stirring constantly.
3. Add the chicken stock and salt and pepper to taste.
4. Cover and pressure cook for five minutes. Reduce pressure and remove the cover.
5. Purée in an electric blender, then pour through a strainer to remove the seeds, or sieve the mixture through a strainer. Return to the cooker.
6. In a small saucepan, melt the butter. Remove from the heat and stir in the flour. Return to the heat and cook for one minute. Slowly add the milk, stirring constantly. Cook until thickened.
7. Stir the white sauce into the soup and cook over a low heat for three minutes.
8. Add the cream and heat through. Do not boil.
9. Serve garnished with chopped parsley and sprinkled with paprika.

Serves 6.

Cream of Onion Soup

2 lb (1 kg) onions
2 cloves garlic, minced
3 tablespoons (60 g) butter
3 cups (750 ml) beef stock
salt
freshly ground black pepper

2 tablespoons flour
½ cup (125 ml) milk
2 cups (500 ml) cream
grated cheese
croutons

1. Peel and slice the onions and sauté in the butter with garlic in an open pressure cooker until golden brown.
2. Add the stock and salt and pepper to taste. Pressure cook for three minutes. Reduce the pressure and open.
3. Mix the flour with the milk then stir into the cream.
4. Add to the soup and blend thoroughly. Heat through but do not boil.
5. Serve garnished with grated cheese and croutons.

Serves 6.

Tomato Soup

2 small onions
2 slices bacon
3 tablespoons (60 g) butter
1 cup chopped celery
2 tablespoons chopped parsley
1 clove garlic, minced
2 lb (1 kg) tomatoes, chopped

6 cups (1½ liters) chicken stock
1 bay leaf
salt
freshly ground black pepper
sour cream
chopped fresh basil

1. Peel and chop the onions.
2. Chop the bacon and heat in the open pressure cooker with the butter until the butter melts.
3. Add the onions, celery, parsley, garlic and tomatoes and cook over a low heat, stirring frequently for two minutes.
4. Add the chicken stock, bay leaf and salt and pepper to taste. Cover and allow to pressure cook for five minutes. Allow pressure to reduce, and remove the cover.
5. Purée the soup in an electric blender then strain to remove the seeds, or sieve the soup through a strainer. Return to the cooker and heat through.
6. Serve topped with a spoonful of sour cream and garnished with chopped basil.

Serves 6.

Potato and Onion Soup

1½ lb (750 g) potatoes
3 medium onions, chopped
2 cups (500 ml) chicken stock
salt and pepper
2 tablespoons flour

1½ cups (375 ml) milk
1 cup (250 ml) cream
2 tablespoons (40 g) butter
3 tablespoons chopped chives
paprika

1. Peel and dice the potatoes and put into the pressure cooker with the onions and chicken stock. Season well with salt and pepper.
2. Cover and pressure cook for eight minutes.
3. Put the potatoes and onions in the electric blender. Whirl until smooth then return to the pressure cooker.
4. Blend the flour with a little of the milk then add to the rest of the milk. Pour into the potato mixture and bring to a boil, stirring constantly. Reduce heat and simmer for five minutes.
5. Stir in the cream, butter and chives. Heat until the butter is melted. Do not boil.
6. Serve with paprika sprinkled on top of each bowl.

Serves 6.

Carrot Soup

1½ lb (750 g) carrots
2 small onions, chopped
2 tablespoons (40 g) butter
½ teaspoon thyme
¼ teaspoon nutmeg

6 cups (1½ liters) chicken stock
salt
freshly ground black pepper
chopped chives

1. Peel and chop the carrots. If the carrots are very young, do not peel, just chop.
2. Sauté the onions in the butter in the open pressure cooker until transparent.
3. Add the carrots and cook over a low heat for three minutes, stirring frequently.
4. Add the thyme, nutmeg, chicken stock and salt and pepper to taste. Mix well and pressure cook for five minutes.
5. Allow the pressure to reduce, then purée the carrots and onions in an electric blender or sieve through a fine strainer.
6. Return to the cooker and heat through. Serve garnished with chopped chives.

Serves 6.

Artichoke Soup

1½ lb (750 g) Jerusalem artichokes	2 tablespoons flour
1 tablespoon vinegar	⅔ cup (165 ml) milk
2 cups (500 ml) water	1 tablespoon (20 g) butter
2 teaspoons lemon juice	1 egg yolk
salt and black pepper	⅔ cup (165 ml) cream
	chopped chives

1. Peel and quarter the artichokes. Put into a bowl of water with the vinegar until all the artichokes are prepared. Drain.
2. Put the artichokes into the pressure cooker with the water, lemon juice, salt and pepper to taste.
3. Cover and pressure cook for ten minutes. Allow pressure to reduce.
4. Purée the artichokes in the electric blender, then return to the cooker.
5. Blend the flour with the milk and add to the artichokes.
6. Cook, stirring constantly, until the mixture comes to a boil.
7. Reduce the heat and add the butter, stirring until the butter melts.
8. Beat the egg yolk with the cream. Stir into the soup and heat through. Do not boil.
9. Serve garnished with chopped chives.

Serves 6.

Beef Consomme

½ lb (250 g) gravy beef	1 clove garlic, halved
6 cups (1½ liters) beef stock	1 bay leaf
1 medium onion, quartered	salt and black pepper
1 medium carrot, thickly sliced	sherry

1. Cut the beef into small pieces discarding any fat.
2. Put the meat into the pressure cooker with the beef stock, onion, carrot, garlic and bay leaf.
3. Cover and pressure cook for ½ hour. Allow the pressure to reduce and remove the cover.
4. Strain the soup through a fine sieve.
5. Add salt and pepper to taste and a little sherry. Serve immediately.

Serves 6.

Celery Soup

1½ lb (750 g) celery
2 cups (500 ml) chicken stock
salt and pepper
¼ cup flour

1½ cups (375 ml) milk
⅔ cup (165 ml) cream
1½ tablespoons (30 g) butter
chopped parsley

1. Prepare the celery removing the tough strings and cutting into thick slices.
2. Put into the pressure cooker with the chicken stock and salt and pepper to taste.
3. Cover and pressure cook for ten minutes. Allow pressure to reduce.
4. Put the celery into the electric blender and whirl until smooth. Return to the pressure cooker.
5. Blend the flour with a little of the milk, then with the remaining milk. Stir into the celery.
6. Bring to a boil, stirring constantly. Reduce heat and simmer for five minutes.
7. Add the cream and butter and stir until the butter is melted.
8. Serve garnished with chopped parsley.

Serves 6.

Borscht

½ lb (250 g) beets, grated
2 tablespoons vegetable oil
½ lb (250 g) potatoes, chopped
1 medium onion, minced
½ lb (250 g) cabbage, shredded

6 cups (1½ liters) chicken stock
salt and pepper
2 bay leaves
2 tablespoons lemon juice
sour cream

1. Sauté the beets in the vegetable oil in the open pressure cooker for about five minutes.
2. Add the potatoes, onion, cabbage, chicken stock, salt and pepper to taste, bay leaves and lemon juice. Mix thoroughly.
3. Cover and pressure for 20 minutes. Allow pressure to drop, then remove the cover.
4. Serve with a spoonful of sour cream in each dish.

Serves 6.

Onion Soup

½ cup (125 g) butter
8 medium onions, chopped
6 cups (1½ liters) beef stock
freshly ground black pepper

salt
1 cup (250 ml) dry white wine
6 slices French bread, toasted
⅔ cup grated Swiss cheese

1. Melt the butter in the open pressure cooker and sauté the onions for five minutes.
2. Add the beef stock and mix well.
3. Pressure cook for ten minutes.
4. Reduce pressure and season to taste with salt and pepper and add the wine.
5. Pressure cook for another ten minutes.
6. Put a piece of toast in each of six soup bowls. Sprinkle with the grated Swiss cheese.
7. Pour the soup over the French bread and cheese and serve immediately.

Serves 6.

Tomato Vegetable Soup

3 cups (750 ml) beef stock
½ cup (125 g) tomato paste
1 cup (250 ml) tomato purée
1 cup (250 ml) water
1 large potato, chopped
1 medium carrot, chopped

1 stalk celery, chopped
1 medium onion, chopped
4 ripe tomatoes, peeled and chopped
½ sweet green pepper, chopped
1 teaspoon salt
½ teaspoon black pepper

1. Put the beef stock, tomato paste, tomato purée and water into the pressure cooker and stir until thoroughly blended.
2. Add the vegetables, salt and pepper, cover and pressure cook for five minutes. Allow the pressure to drop naturally and serve.

Serves 6.

Cream of Carrot Soup

1½ lb (750 g) carrots
2 small onions, chopped
2 tablespoons (40 g) butter
¼ teaspoon nutmeg
3 cups (750 ml) chicken stock
1½ tablespoons (30 g) butter
1½ tablespoons flour

1¼ cups (300 ml) milk
salt and freshly ground black
  pepper
2 egg yolks
1 cup (250 ml) cream
chopped mint

1. Peel and chop the carrots. If the carrots are very young and tender, do not peel, just chop.
2. Sauté the onions in the butter in the open pressure cooker until transparent.
3. Add the carrots and cook over a low heat for two minutes.
4. Add the nutmeg and chicken stock and pressure cook for eight minutes. Reduce pressure and open.
5. In a small saucepan melt the 1½ tablespoons of butter. Remove from the heat and stir in flour. Return to the heat and cook for one minute. Slowly add the milk and cook over a low heat stirring constantly until thickened. Season to taste with salt and pepper.
6. Pour the carrot mixture into an electric blender and whirl until smooth or press the carrots through a fine sieve. Return to the cooker.
7. Add the white sauce to the carrot mixture. Blend thoroughly.
8. Beat the egg yolks with the cream. Slowly add to the hot soup, stirring constantly. Heat through but do not boil.
9. Serve garnished with chopped mint.

Serves 6-8.

Vegetables

Green Beans

1 lb (500 g) green beans
1 cup (250 ml) water
1 teaspoon salt
1 tablespoon (20 g) butter
1 tablespoon lemon juice
freshly ground black pepper

1. String the beans if necessary but do not cut the beans.
2. Pour the water into the pressure cooker with the salt and bring to a boil.
3. Put the beans on a rack or trivet in the cooker. Cover and pressure cook for three minutes (or less if you like them crunchy). Reduce the pressure rapidly by running cold water over the lid. Uncover and drain.
4. Melt the butter in the pressure cooker and add the lemon juice and black pepper to taste.
5. Put the beans back in the cooker and toss in the lemon butter over a medium heat for one minute. Serve immediately.

Serves 4.

Lima Beans with Ham

1 lb (500 g) dried lima beans
¾ lb (375 g) ham
1 tablespoon vegetable oil
1¼ cups (300 ml) water

1½ teaspoons salt
1 medium onion, chopped
1 tablespoon brown sugar
chopped parsley

1. Soak the lima beans in enough water to cover overnight. Drain.
2. Heat the vegetable oil in the open pressure cooker and sauté the ham over a low heat for three minutes, stirring frequently.
3. Add the lima beans, water, salt, onion and brown sugar. Mix well.
4. Cover and pressure cook for ½ hour. Allow pressure to drop.
5. Serve garnished with chopped parsley.

Serves 6-8.

Mashed Vegetables

3 medium potatoes
2 medium carrots
¼ lb (125 g) canned pumpkin
1 cooking apple
1 small onion

1 teaspoon salt
¼ teaspoon black pepper
2 tablespoons chopped parsley
½ cup (125 ml) chicken stock
2 tablespoons (40 g) butter

1. Peel the potatoes, carrots, pumpkin, apple and onion and cut into chunks. Put into the pressure cooker on top of the rack or trivet.
2. Sprinkle on the salt, pepper and parsley. Pour on the chicken stock.
3. Cover and pressure cook for three minutes. Reduce the pressure by running cold water over the lid. Uncover and drain. Remove the trivet or rack.
4. Mash the vegetables with the butter. Season to taste with salt and pepper.

Serves 4.

Chinese Vegetables

3 tablespoons vegetable oil
¼ lb (125 g) fresh mushrooms,
  sliced
2 small onions, sliced
3 stalks celery, sliced
1 clove garlic, minced
½ cup chopped celery leaves

1 sweet green pepper, chopped
1 cup (250 ml) beef stock
1 cup green beans, sliced
1 tablespoon soy sauce
½ teaspoon salt
1 tablespoon cornstarch
3 tablespoons cold water

1. Heat the oil in the pressure cooker and sauté the mushrooms, onions, celery, garlic, celery leaves and green pepper for two minutes over a medium heat stirring constantly.
2. Add the beef stock, green beans, soy sauce and salt.
3. Cover and pressure cook for two minutes. Reduce the pressure rapidly by running cold water over the lid. Uncover.
4. Blend the cornstarch with the cold water and stir into the vegetables. Stirring over a low heat, cook until thickened and clear.

Serves 4.

Broccoli French Style

1 lb (500 g) broccoli
½ cup (125 ml) water
1 bay leaf
2 teaspoons grated lemon rind

2 thin slices lemon
1 clove garlic, minced
salt
freshly ground black pepper

1. Wash and drain the broccoli. Remove the leaves from the stalks and cut the stems off about one inch (2½ cm) from the stalks.
2. Put the water, bay leaf, grated lemon rind, lemon slices, garlic and salt and pepper to taste in the pressure cooker and bring to a boil.
3. Put the broccoli on a rack or trivet, cover and pressure cook for three minutes. Reduce the pressure rapidly by running cold water over the lid. Uncover.
4. Put the broccoli on a serving platter. Remove the bay leaf and lemon slices and pour the stock over the broccoli.

Serves 4.

Carrots with Orange

1 lb (500 g) carrots
3 tablespoons thawed frozen
   orange juice concentrate
3 tablespoons (60 g) butter

1½ tablespoons honey
½ teaspoon grated fresh ginger
½ teaspoon salt

1. Peel the carrots only if necessary. Cut into halves lengthwise. If large, cut into quarters lengthwise.
2. Put the orange juice concentrate, butter, honey, ginger and salt into the pressure cooker and stir until the butter is melted.
3. Put the carrots on a rack or trivet, cover and pressure cook for three minutes. Reduce the pressure rapidly by running cold water over the lid. Uncover.
4. Put the carrots on a serving dish and pour the orange mixture over them.

Serves 4.

Beet Salad

2 lb (1 kg) beets
½ cup (125 ml) cider vinegar
½ cup (125 ml) water
¼ cup (65 ml) vegetable oil
1½ teaspoons dried dill
1 teaspoon salt

½ teaspoon black pepper
1 cup (250 g) sour cream
2 tablespoons freeze dried onions
1 tablespoon chopped chives
½ teaspoon dried dill
salt and pepper

1. Scrub the beets but leave the root and the stem on.
2. Put on a rack or trivet in the pressure cooker and add the vinegar, water, oil, 1½ teaspoons dried dill, salt and pepper.
3. Cover and pressure cook for ten minutes. Reduce the pressure rapidly by running cold water over the lid. Uncover.
4. Put the beets into a bowl and pour the liquid from the cooker over them. Chill for several hours.
5. Scoop out a hollow in the beets leaving a thick shell. Cut a third of the pulp into small cubes. (Reserve the other two-thirds for other uses.)
6. Mix together the sour cream, dried onions, chopped chives, dill, salt and pepper to taste and the diced beets. Pile into the shells and chill for several hours before serving.

Serves 4-6.

Beans Vinaigrette

1 lb (500 g) green beans	1 tablespoon chopped onion
1 cup (250 ml) water	1 clove garlic, halved
½ teaspoon salt	4 sprigs parsley
⅓ cup (85 ml) vegetable oil	½ teaspoon salt
2 tablespoons white vinegar	½ teaspoon black pepper
1½ tablespoons malt vinegar	½ teaspoon powdered mustard

1. Wash the beans and remove the strings and the ends.
2. Pour the water into the pressure cooker with the salt. Bring to a boil.
3. Put the beans on a rack or trivet and cover. Pressure cook for two minutes. Reduce the pressure by running cold water over the lid. Uncover and put the beans into a shallow dish.
4. Put the remaining ingredients in the electric blender and whirl until smooth. Pour over the beans. Either serve warm or chilled.

Serves 4.

Tomatoes

1 lb (500 g) small firm tomatoes
1¼ cups (300 ml) water
1 teaspoon salt
chopped fresh basil
salt and freshly ground black
   pepper

1. Wash the tomatoes well.
2. Pour the water into the pressure cooker with the salt and bring to a boil.
3. Put the tomatoes on a rack or trivet and cover. Cook only until the regulator begins to rock. Reduce the pressure rapidly by running cold water over the lid. Uncover.
4. Serve sprinkled with chopped basil and seasoned with salt and pepper.

Serves 4.

Brussels Sprouts

1 lb (500 g) Brussels sprouts
1¼ cups (300 ml) water
1 teaspoon salt
1½ tablespoons (30 g) butter
2 teaspoons lemon juice
salt and freshly ground black
　pepper

1. Wash the Brussels sprouts well and remove wilted outer leaves.
2. Pour the water into the pressure cooker with the salt and bring to a boil.
3. Put the Brussels sprouts on a rack or trivet, cover and pressure cook for three minutes. Reduce the pressure rapidly by running cold water over the lid. Uncover.
4. Drain the Brussels sprouts and remove the rack or trivet.
5. Add the butter and lemon juice and stir gently until the butter is melted and the sprouts are well-coated. Season generously with salt and pepper.

Serves 4.

Corn on the Cob

4 cobs of corn
1¼ cups (300 ml) water
1 teaspoon salt
butter
salt and pepper

1. Remove the husks and silk from the corn.
2. Pour the water into the pressure cooker with the salt and bring to a boil.
3. Arrange the corn on a rack or trivet and cover. Pressure cook for 3-5 minutes depending on the tenderness of the corn. Reduce the pressure quickly by running cold water over the lid. Uncover.
4. Serve the corn with butter, salt and pepper.

Serves 4.

Potatoes

1 lb (500 g) small new potatoes
1¼ cups (300 ml) water
1 teaspoon salt
2 tablespoons (40 g) butter
2 tablespoons chopped parsley
salt and black pepper

1. Wash the potatoes thoroughly.
2. Pour the water into the pressure cooker with the salt and bring to a boil.
3. Put the potatoes on a rack or trivet and cover. Pressure cook for four minutes. Reduce the pressure rapidly by running cold water on the lid. Uncover.
4. Take the potatoes out of the cooker and discard the water.
5. Melt the butter with the parsley in the cooker. Return the potatoes and toss gently to ensure that they are well-coated. Season generously with salt and freshly ground black pepper.

Serves 4.

Spinach

1½ lb (750 g) fresh spinach
butter
salt
freshly ground black pepper

1. Wash the spinach several times in cold water. Remove the central white stem. Drain the spinach, then tear into pieces.
2. Put the spinach in the pressure cooker, cover and cook just until the regulator starts to rock. Reduce the pressure rapidly by running cold water over the lid. (When putting the spinach in the cooker be sure it is not more than two-thirds full.) Remove the cover.
3. Drain the spinach, stir in some butter and season well with salt and pepper.

Serves 4.

Peas

1 lb (500 g) peas
1¼ cups (300 ml) water
1 teaspoon salt
1 tablespoon chopped mint
2 tablespoons (40 g) butter
1 teaspoon sugar
salt and pepper

1. Shell the peas.
2. Pour the water into the pressure cooker with the salt and chopped mint. Bring to a boil.
3. Put the peas on a rack or trivet, cover and pressure cook for three minutes. Reduce the pressure rapidly by running cold water over the lid. Uncover.
4. Drain the peas discarding the water.
5. Melt the butter in the pressure cooker with the sugar. Toss the peas in the melted butter. Season to taste with salt and pepper and serve immediately.

Serves 4.

Peppers

1 lb (500 g) sweet green or red peppers
1¼ cups (300 ml) water
1 teaspoon salt
2 tablespoons (40 g) butter

1 clove garlic, minced
1 small onion, minced
salt and pepper

1. Remove the core and seeds from the peppers. Cut into squares.
2. Pour the water into the pressure cooker with the salt and bring to a boil.
3. Put the peppers on a rack or trivet and cover. Pressure cook for four minutes. Reduce the pressure rapidly by running cold water over the lid. Uncover.
4. Transfer the peppers to a warm dish and discard the water.
5. Sauté the garlic and onion in the butter in the pressure cooker for one minute.
6. Add the peppers and toss gently to ensure that the peppers are thoroughly coated with the butter. Season to taste with salt and pepper.

Serves 4.

Onions

1 lb (500 g) small onions
1¼ cups (300 ml) water
1 teaspoon salt
2 tablespoons (40 g) butter
1 clove garlic, minced
salt and freshly ground black
    pepper

1. Peel the onions and leave whole.
2. Pour the water into the pressure cooker with the salt and bring to a boil.
3. Put the onions on a rack or trivet, cover and pressure cook for four minutes. Reduce the pressure rapidly by running cold water over the lid. Uncover.
4. Remove the onions and discard the water.
5. Melt the butter in the cooker and sauté the garlic for ½ minute.
6. Return the onions to the cooker and toss gently in the garlic butter. Season to taste with salt and pepper.

Serves 4-6.

Parsnips

1 lb (500 g) parsnips
1¼ cups (300 ml) water
1 teaspoon salt
1½ tablespoons (30 g) butter
salt and freshly ground black
    pepper

1. Peel and slice or dice the parsnips.
2. Pour the water into the pressure cooker with the salt and bring to a boil.
3. Put the parsnips into the water (no rack or trivet needed), cover and pressure cook for four minutes. Reduce the pressure rapidly by running cold water over the lid. Uncover, and drain.
4. Stir the butter into the parsnips until melted. Season to taste with salt and pepper.

Serves 4.

Leeks

1 lb (500 g) leeks
1¼ cups (300 ml) water
1 teaspoon salt
2 tablespoons (40 g) butter
chopped parsley
salt and black pepper

1. Wash the leeks and trim the ends. Cut in half lengthwise if large.
2. Pour the water into the pressure cooker with the salt and bring to a boil.
3. Put the leeks onto a rack or trivet, cover and pressure cook for four minutes. Reduce the pressure rapidly by running cold water over the lid. Remove the lid.
4. Put the leeks on a warm serving dish. Discard the water.
5. Melt the butter with the parsley in the cooker. Pour over the leeks, then season generously with salt and freshly ground black pepper.

Serves 4.

Marrow

1 lb (500 g) marrow
1¼ cups (300 ml) water
1 teaspoon salt
2 tablespoons (40 g) butter
1 tablespoon chopped chives
salt and black pepper

1. Peel the marrow and cut into thick slices.
2. Pour the water into the pressure cooker with the salt and bring to a boil.
3. Put the marrow slices on a rack or trivet, cover and pressure cook for 3-4 minutes. Reduce the pressure rapidly by running cold water over the lid. Uncover.
4. Put the marrow on a warm serving dish. Discard the water.
5. Melt the butter with the chives in the cooker. Pour over the marrow and season to taste with salt and pepper.

Serves 4.

Chicory

1 lb (500 g) chicory
2 tablespoons (40 g) butter
2 teaspoons lemon juice
1 tablespoon chopped parsley
salt and black pepper
⅔ cup (165 ml) water

1. Wash and dry the chicory well.
2. Melt the butter in the pressure cooker with the lemon juice, parsley and salt and pepper to taste.
3. Add the chicory and coat thoroughly with the butter mixture.
4. Add the water, cover and pressure cook for four minutes. Reduce the pressure rapidly by running cold water over the lid.

Serves 4.

Zucchini

1 lb (500 g) zucchini
1¼ cups (300 ml) water
1 teaspoon salt
2 tablespoons (40 g) butter
1 clove garlic, minced
salt and black pepper

1. Cut the top and bottom from the zucchini and cut in half lengthwise.
2. Pour the water into the pressure cooker with the salt and bring to a boil.
3. Put the zucchini on a rack or trivet, cover and pressure cook for 1½-2 minutes. Reduce the pressure quickly by running cold water over the lid. Remove the lid.
4. Put the zucchini on a dish and keep warm. Discard the water.
5. Melt the butter in the pressure cooker and sauté the garlic for ½ minute.
6. Add the zucchini and toss gently to coat thoroughly. Season to taste with salt and pepper.

Serves 4.

Cauliflower

1 medium cauliflower
1¼ cups (300 ml) water
1 teaspoon salt
⅔ cup dried bread crumbs
⅔ cup grated Parmesan cheese
⅓ cup (85 ml) melted butter

1. Divide the cauliflower into flowerets.
2. Pour the water and salt into the pressure cooker and bring to a boil.
3. Put the cauliflower onto a rack or trivet, cover and pressure cook for three minutes. Reduce the pressure rapidly by running cold water over the lid. Remove the lid.
4. Put the cauliflower into a buttered shallow baking dish.
5. Mix together the bread crumbs and cheese and sprinkle on top of the cauliflower. Drip the butter on top.
6. Bake in a 400°F (200°C) oven until golden brown.

Serves 4-6.

Celery

1 lb (500 g) celery stalks
1¼ cups (300 ml) water
1 teaspoon salt
3 tablespoons (60 g) butter
2 teaspoons lemon juice
salt and black pepper

1. Wash the celery and remove any coarse strings. Cut into one-inch (2½-cm) lengths.
2. Pour the water into the pressure cooker with the salt and bring to a boil.
3. Put the celery on a rack or trivet, cover and pressure cook for four minutes. Reduce the pressure quickly by running cold water over the lid. Remove the lid.
4. Remove the celery and rack or trivet from the cooker and discard the water.
5. Melt the butter in the cooker with the lemon juice.
6. Add the celery and toss to coat thoroughly. Season to taste with salt and pepper.

Serves 4.

Cabbage

½ medium cabbage
1¼ cups (300 ml) water
1 teaspoon salt
2 tablespoons (40 g) butter
1 tablespoon lemon juice
salt and pepper

1. Shred the cabbage uniformly.
2. Pour the water and salt into the pressure cooker and bring to a boil.
3. Put the cabbage on a rack or trivet and cover. Pressure cook for two minutes. Reduce the pressure rapidly by running cold water over the lid. Uncover and drain.
4. Melt the butter in the pressure cooker and stir in the lemon juice and salt and pepper to taste.
5. Add the cabbage and toss in the lemon butter. Serve immediately.

Serves 4-6.

Carrots

1 lb (500 g) carrots
1¼ cups (300 ml) water
1 teaspoon salt
1 tablespoon (20 g) butter
1 tablespoon honey
½ teaspoon grated lemon rind
salt and pepper

1. If the carrots are young, do not peel. If old, peel and cut into thick slices.
2. Pour the water into the pressure cooker with the salt. Bring to a boil.
3. Put the carrots on a rack or trivet and cover. Pressure cook for four minutes. Reduce the pressure quickly by running cold water over the lid. Uncover and drain.
4. Melt the butter in the pressure cooker. Add the honey and lemon rind. Stir until the honey is melted.
5. Add the carrots and toss in the honey/butter mixture ensuring they are well-coated. Season to taste with salt and pepper.

Serves 4.

Beets

1 lb (500 g) beets
2½ cups (625 ml) water
1 teaspoon salt
freshly ground black pepper
sour cream
chopped chives

1. Scrub the beets but do not peel.
2. Pour the water into the pressure cooker with the salt.
3. Add the beets, cover and pressure cook for ten minutes. (If the beets are large, increase the water to four cups and the cooking time to thirty minutes.) Reduce the pressure quickly by running cold water over the lid. Uncover and drain.
4. Allow the beets to cool slightly, then peel and slice.
5. Sprinkle with black pepper and top with sour cream and chopped chives.

Serves 4.

Broccoli

1 lb (500 g) broccoli
1¼ cups (300 ml) water
1 teaspoon salt
¼ cup (65 g) butter, melted
½ cup bread crumbs
½ cup grated Cheddar cheese
¼ cup grated Parmesan cheese

1. Trim the coarse stems and outer leaves from the broccoli.
2. Pour the water into the pressure cooker with the salt and bring to a boil.
3. Put the broccoli on a rack or trivet, cover and pressure cook for two to three minutes. Reduce the pressure quickly by running cold water over the lid. Remove the lid and drain. Put the broccoli into a heat-proof dish.
4. Mix together the butter, bread crumbs, Cheddar and Parmesan cheeses. Sprinkle on top of the broccoli. Put under a hot broiler or in a hot oven until the top is golden brown.

Asparagus with Hollandaise Sauce

1 lb (500 g) asparagus
1¼ cups (300 ml) water
1 teaspoon salt

Hollandaise Sauce:
4 egg yolks
2 tablespoons lemon juice
¼ teaspoon salt
⅛ teaspoon white pepper
½ cup (125 ml) hot melted butter

1. Trim the hard white ends from the asparagus. Tie into bundles of 5 or 6.
2. Pour the water into the pressure cooker with the salt and bring to a boil.
3. If possible, stand the asparagus upright in the cooker. Cover and pressure cook for two to four minutes depending on the size. Reduce the pressure rapidly by running cold water over the lid. Remove the lid and drain.
4. To make the Hollandaise sauce, put the egg yolks, lemon juice, salt and pepper into the electric blender. Whirl on high speed for ½ minute.
5. Continue blending on high speed while adding the hot butter a drop at a time until it begins to thicken, then add a bit more quickly. Whirl until thick and smooth.
6. Serve the asparagus with the sauce poured over the top .

Serves 3-4.

Eggplant

    1 large eggplant
    1¼ cups (300 ml) water
    1 clove garlic, minced
    1 teaspoon salt
    ¼ teaspoon black pepper
    2 tablespoons (40 g) butter
    1 tablespoon chopped parsley

1. Cut the eggplant into slices and sprinkle generously with salt. Set aside for ½ hour. Pour off any liquid.
2. Pour the water into the pressure cooker with the garlic, salt and pepper. Bring to a boil.
3. Add the eggplant slices, cover and pressure cook for three minutes. Bring the pressure down rapidly by running cold water over the lid. Uncover and drain the eggplant. Remove the eggplant to a serving platter.
4. Melt the butter in the pressure cooker. Add the parsley and stir for one minute over a low heat. Pour over the eggplant and serve immediately.

Serves 3-4.

Artichokes

    2 Globe artichokes
    1¼ cups (300 ml) water
    1 teaspoon salt
    ¼ cup (65 g) butter
    2 tablespoons lemon juice
    ½ teaspoon salt
    ¼ teaspoon freshly ground black
      pepper

1. Trim the outer leaves from the artichokes and cut off the tough part of the stem.
2. Pour the water into the pressure cooker with the salt and bring to a boil.
3. Put the artichokes into the cooker on top of a rack or trivet.
4. Cover and pressure cook for 5-6 minutes. Reduce the pressure rapidly by running cold water over the lid. Remove the artichokes and drain.
5. While the artichokes are cooking, heat together the butter, lemon juice, salt and pepper in a small saucepan. Serve with the artichokes.

Serves 2.

General Hints

Pressure Cooking

When the pressure must be reduced rapidly, run cold water over the lid of the cooker.

When the pressure is to be reduced gradually, remove the pressure cooker from the heat and leave at room temperature.

Never fill the pressure cooker more than two-thirds full.

When you are steaming a dish, keep the basin above the water resting on a rack or trivet.

Calculate the cooking time from when the Pressure Regulator begins to jiggle.

Do not remove the Pressure Regulator until the pressure has dropped.

Read the instructions thoroughly for your particular pressure cooker before attempting to cook anything in it.

Index

HL/IM—C8000—1/124